SHAMANISM

THE
ELEMENT
LIBRARY

SHAMANISM

NEVILL DRURY

ELEMENT
Shaftesbury, Dorset
Rockport, Massachusetts
Brisbane, Queensland

© Element Books Limited 1996
Text © Nevill Drury

Published in Great Britain 1996 by
ELEMENT BOOKS LIMITED
SHAFTESBURY, DORSET SP7 8BP

Published in the USA in 1996 by
ELEMENT INC.
PO Box 830, Rockport, MA 01966

Published in Australia in 1996 by
ELEMENT BOOKS LIMITED for
JACARANDA WILEY LIMITED
33 Park Road, Milton, Brisbane, 4046

Designed and created by
THE BRIDGEWATER BOOK COMPANY
Art Director *Peter Bridgewater*
Designer *Jane Lanaway*
Editor *Fiona Corbridge*
Managing Editor *Anne Townley*
Picture Research *Vanessa Fletcher*
Page Make-up *Chris Lanaway*

Printed in Hong Kong by
Midas Printing Ltd

British Library Cataloguing-in-Publication Data available

Library of Congress Cataloging-in-Publication
Data available

ISBN 1–85230–794–3

❖

CONTENTS

INTRODUCTION

Our mental picture of shamanism is often a vague collage of images of enigmatic medicine men or sorceresses. Shamans, however, have many roles. They may indeed be healers, able to conquer the spirits of disease, or sorcerers, skilled in harnessing spirits as allies for magical purposes. They are also 'soul travellers', who through entering a condition of trance are mysteriously able to journey to sacred places and convey messages to humankind on matters of cosmic intent. They may be 'psychic detectives', able to recover lost possessions. At other times the shaman may seem to have the function of a priest, acting as an intermediary between the gods of creation and the more familiar realm of everyday domestic affairs. Whatever the specific role, the shaman is one who universally commands awe and respect: he or she is a person who can journey to other worlds and return with revelations from the gods.

Shamanism is thus a visionary tradition, an ancient practice of utilizing altered states of consciousness to contact the spirits of the natural world. This is where it begins to touch our modern lives. At a time when we are all becoming increasingly aware of our environment and the fragility of ecological balance, the essential call of shamanism is clear: we should respect the sanctity of Nature. Shamanism reminds us that our destinies on Earth are intertwined and interdependent. For us, as for the ancients, the voice of the shaman offers a powerful and optimistic message.

RIGHT *A Huichol Indian yarn painting, showing the dangers facing a prospective shaman on the path of initiation.*

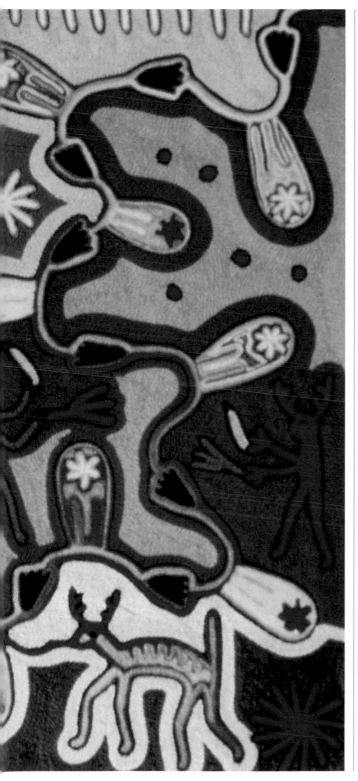

Eskimo shaman's mask.

Shaman performing a bird dance.

Shaman starting a spirit-journey.

1

ANIMISM AND BEYOND

*Shamanism is a visionary approach to nature and the cosmos.
Underlying all forms of shamanism is the belief that the universe is
alive with gods and spirits. The oldest paintings in the world are Palaeolithic
cave paintings made in about 30,000 BC. In 1940, caves were discovered at
Lascaux in France containing many fine pictures of animals, such as this
running horse, on the walls.*

ANIMISM AND TOTEMISM

To understand the essence of shamanism it is first necessary to consider the earliest forms of religious expression, since we can then obtain a framework, or context, for the rise of shamanic beliefs and practices.

Prehistoric Graves

The earliest tangible manifestations of Man's religious awareness have been found in prehistoric cave sites located in Europe and Central Asia. A Neanderthal grave discovered in Uzbekistan revealed that a circle of ibex horns had been placed reverently around the body of a dead child. In a cave at Le Moustier in France, a dead youth was buried with his head resting on his right arm, as if asleep, supported by a pillow of flint flakes. A selection of tools and bones of animals, left close to hand, suggested strongly that these implements could serve the youth in some future life.

It is possible that even at this early stage of human development, Neanderthal man believed in a world in which spirit beings inhabited animals, rocks and trees, and that his role as a hunter would continue in some sort of afterlife.

Art and Magic

By the Upper Palaeolithic Era, there is a clear indication that Man had begun to think in magical terms. The noted scholar Abbé Henri Breuil refers to the prehistoric cave and mural art of Western Europe as follows:

>﹢﹣
>
> *Animals are represented pierced with symbolical arrows (bison and ibexes at Niaux; horses at Lascaux), clay models are riddled with spent marks (at Montespan, a headless lion and bear, which seem to have received new skins at various times): facts which evoke the idea of sympathetic magic. The numerous pregnant women and men closely pursuing their women suggest the idea of fertility magic. The deliberate alteration of the essential features of certain animals seems to indicate taboos. Human figures dressed up in animal or grotesque masks evoke the dancing and initiation ceremonies of living people or represent the sorcerers or gods of the Upper Palaeolithic.*[1]
>
>﹢﹣

The Sorcerer

One of the most characteristic examples of magical cave art was discovered in the Franco-Cantabrian cave of Les Trois-Frères. Some 15,000 years old, the cave drawings depict a hunter-sorcerer armed with a bow and disguised as a bison, amidst a herd of wild beasts. Another example of a sorcerer wearing horned headgear to deceive his prey was also found at the same site.

From early times, religion, art and magic seem to have been intertwined. The sorcerer was a master of wild animals – able to control their fate through his hunting magic, adept at disguises, and a practitioner of animal sacrifice. He learned to mimic the animals and in turn based his dances on their movements, and felt he had developed a psychic bond with them. In this way, the Palaeolithic hunter-sorcerer was a precursor of the archetypal shaman, who had animal familiars, clan totems, and believed that consciousness could be transformed into an animal form.

The pioneering English anthropologist Sir Edward Tylor (1832–1917) gave a name to the earliest phase of magical and religious thinking, calling it animism, after the Greek word *anima*, meaning 'soul'.

BELOW LEFT
A painting of a sorcerer from the cave of Les Trois-Frères in France.

❖

BELOW *Native American rock painting of a bear shaman and assistant, with the thunderbird above.*

THE SHAMANIC VOCATION

ABOVE *Eskimo salmon mask and* BELOW *hair seal mask. The human face on each mask represents the creature's spirit.*

Shamanism is really applied animism, or animism in practice. Because Nature is alive with gods and spirits, and because all aspects of the cosmos are perceived as interconnected (the universe consisting of a veritable network of energies, forms and vibrations), the shaman is required as an intermediary between the different planes of being.

The idea of a universe alive with spirits is brought home in the journals of Danish explorer and anthropologist Knud Rasmussen (1879–1933), who undertook an epic three-year journey in the American Arctic regions. Rasmussen, whose own grandmother was part-Eskimo, had a fine rapport with the polar Eskimos and was very interested when an Iglulik shaman told him:

❖

'The greatest peril of life lies in the fact that human food consists entirely of souls. All the creatures that we have to kill and eat, all those that we have to strike down and destroy to make clothes for ourselves have souls, souls that do not perish with the body and which must therefore be pacified lest they should revenge themselves on us for taking away their bodies.'[2]

❖

ABOVE *A 1903 portrait of the Danish explorer and anthropologist Knud Rasmussen. Rasmussen learned much about the spiritual beliefs and traditions of the Eskimos during his 1921–1924 expedition.*

❖

RIGHT *Modern-day Eskimos on Baffin Island still use traditional fishing methods.*

❖

Who is a Shaman?

We can define a shaman as a person who is able to perceive this world of souls, spirits and gods, and who, in a state of ecstatic trance, is able to travel among them, gaining special knowledge of that supernatural realm. He or she is ever alert to the intrinsic perils of human existence, of the magical forces which lie waiting to trap the unwary, or which give rise to disease, famine or misfortune. But the shaman also takes the role of an active intermediary – a negotiator in both directions.

How do People Become Shamans?

Shamans are called to their vocation in different ways. For some it is a matter of ancestral lineage or hereditary bonds establishing the person in that position. Sometimes a would-be shaman seeks initiation from one already established in this role. In other cases it seems almost as if the spirits have chosen the shaman, rather than the other way around. These are the 'greater shamans': those who have been called spontaneously through dreams or mystical visions to embody supernatural power. Those who have simply inherited their role are regarded as 'lesser shamans' and hold a lower status in society, especially among the people of Siberia and Arctic North America.

To begin with, as children or young adults, shamans are often of a nervous disposition and may seem strangely withdrawn from society. As anthropologist Ralph Linton notes:

The shaman as a child usually shows marked introvert tendencies. When these inclinations become manifest they are encouraged by society. The budding shaman often wanders off and spends a long time by himself. He is rather anti-social in his attitudes and is frequently seized by mysterious illnesses of one sort or another.[3]

The Chukchee peoples of Siberia believe that a future shaman can be recognized by 'the

ABOVE *Chukchee women and the family's Leika dogs by their deerskin tent home.*

look in the eyes, which are not directed towards a listener during conversation, but seem fixed on something beyond. The eyes also have a strange quality of light, a peculiar brightness which allows them to see spirits and those things hidden from an ordinary person.'[4] Waldemar Bogoras, who studied the Chukchee at first hand, provides a context for this occurrence: 'The shamanistic call may come during some great misfortune, dangerous and protracted illness, sudden loss of family or property. Then the person, having no other services, turns to the spirits and claims their assistance.'[5]

LEFT *The Chukchee also traditionally used reindeer skin as protective clothing for snowy weather.*

A Mental Illness?

Much has been made of the idea that shamanism is born of crisis and disease, and it has also been compared with schizophrenia. Julian Silverman, who is a leading advocate of this view, feels that the main difference between schizophrenics and shamans is that shamans are 'institutionally supported' in their state of mental derangement while modern society, for the most part, regards schizophrenia as an aberration. He believes that there is a striking parallel between the two phenomena and quotes a psychiatric description of schizophrenic states to make his point:

The experience which the patient undergoes is of the most awesome, universal character; he seems to be living in the midst of a struggle between personified cosmic forces of good and evil, surrounded by animistically enlivened natural objects which are engaged in ominous performances that it is terribly necessary – and impossible – to understand.[6]

However, a clear distinction obviously needs to be made at this point. While shamans and schizophrenics share the ability to move in and out of different mental states, the shaman has gradually learned how to integrate the different realms of consciousness, thereby bringing matters firmly under control. The noted scholar of comparative religion, Mircea Eliade, indicates:

The primitive magician, the medicine man, or the shaman is not only a sick man; he is, above all, a sick man who has been cured, who has succeeded in curing himself. Often when the shaman's or medicine man's vocation is revealed through an illness or epileptoid attack, the initiation of the candidate is equivalent to a cure.[7]

RIGHT *Patients in an Armenian psychiatric hospital.*

❖❖

Eliade also elaborates on this point in his book *Birth and Rebirth*:

The shamans and mystics of primitive societies are considered – and rightly – to be superior beings; their magico-religious powers also find expression in an extension of their mental capacities. The shaman is the man who knows and remembers, that is, who understands the mysteries of life and death.[8]

Clearly, there is more involved than just psychological aberration or disease. Because epilepsy and schizophrenia are regarded in primitive societies as manifestations of the spirit world, it is not surprising that people suffering from these conditions may later become worthwhile shamans. But these people are special because they are open to the world of spirits and have learned to converse with them and manifest their presence, not simply because they are sick. It is only the person who has learned to master the inner worlds who can become accepted as a true shaman. Harnessing the power is everything: the crisis, or disease, thus becomes an initiation.

Control of the Supernatural

Shamans are very much expected to exhibit control of the supernatural powers which interfere with human life. This includes procuring game animals at times when the hunt appears to be failing, driving away evil spirits, obtaining good weather, and curing the sick. The Eskimo shaman, for example, has to journey in trance to the bottom of the sea to propitiate Sedna, the goddess of the sea. Sedna controls the sea mammals which provide food, fuel and skins for clothing, but she also unleashes most of the misfortune that the Eskimo experiences. As William Lessa and Evon Vogt explain:

These misfortunes are due to misdeeds and offences committed by men and they gather in dirt and impurity over the body of the goddess. It is necessary for the shaman to go through a dangerous ordeal to reach the sea goddess at the bottom of the sea. He must then stroke her hair and report the difficulties of his people. The goddess replies that breaches of taboos have caused their misfortunes. Whereupon the shaman returns for the mass confession from all the people who have committed misdeeds. Presumably when all sins are confessed, the sea goddess releases the game, returns lost souls, cures illnesses, and generally makes the world right with the Eskimos again.[9]

Journey to Other Realms

A distinguishing feature of shamanism, then, is the journey of the soul. It is because the shaman can project consciousness to other realms that he or she is called a 'technician of the sacred' or a 'master of ecstasy'. It is this capacity to venture consciously among the spirits and return with sacred information for the benefit of society, that is all-important.

ABOVE *The Eskimo sea goddess Sedna controls the seals which are used for food and fuel.*

RIGHT *An Eskimo hunter. Shamans are responsible for ensuring there are enough animals to hunt.*

THE JOURNEY OF THE SOUL

In one sense, as we have seen, shamanism can be regarded as a controlled act of mental dissociation. It is as if the practitioner is able to travel in soul-body to other realms of existence: harnessing familiar spirits, perhaps encountering spirits of death or disease, meeting with ancestor or creator gods, and sometimes even participating in the mythic drama of the Creation itself.

This act of dissociation can come about in many ways. As we will see in subsequent chapters of this book, sometimes sacred psychedelic plants provide the impetus for the shamanic journey. At other times the spirit quest comes about following periods of fasting, sensory deprivation, meditative focusing, chanting, through the beating of drums, or through a particular response to a dream.

Pakistan

The *dehar* shaman among the Kalash Kafirs of Pakistan, for example, enters a trance state by standing immovably, relaxing and then focusing attention on a ceremonial altar to such an extent that every external element in the field of vision is excluded. The shaman then begins to shiver, jerks spasmodically, and enters an altered state of consciousness.

Singapore

Singaporean shamanic candidates (mostly recent arrivals from China) become a *dang-ki* by displaying spontaneous signs of possession during temple ceremonies and then meditating on well-known *shen* divinities until the dissociational state is fully developed.

Indonesia

Among the Menangkabau, in Indonesia, it is considered that the life-force, or *sumangat*, leaves the body in dreams or during states of sickness, and that the task of the *dukun*, or shaman, is to counteract the hostile influence of evil spirits during the out-of-the-body state. Here the *dukun* summons friendly spirits through a smoke offering, lies down on the ground covered by a blanket, begins to tremble, then projects consciousness into the mystical realm of the spirit world.

Meanwhile, in the Mentawei Islands near Sumatra, shamans dance until they fall into a state of trance. They are then borne up into the sky in a boat carried by eagles where they meet sky spirits and ask them for remedies to treat disease.

Arctic Regions

Traditional Eskimo shamans work themselves into a state of ecstasy by utilizing the energy of a drumbeat and involving spirit helpers. Some Eskimos lace their arms and legs tightly to their bodies to hasten the release of the inner light-force on the 'spirit flight', or *ilimarneq*. Knud Rasmussen, the Danish explorer, provides us with the definitive account of an Eskimo spirit-journey.

OPPOSITE *A herd of horses in Mongolia. Shamans must protect the tribe's animals from evil spirits.*

❖❖

BELOW *Shamans performing a ritual dance for the winter solstice festival, northern Pakistan.*

Eskimo Spirit-Journey

The particular incident described in Rasmussen's *Report of the Fifth Thule Expedition 1921–1924*, involved breaches of taboos which had invoked the wrath of the sea goddess. The shaman's role was to intercede on the community's behalf, travelling in soul-body to the bottom of the sea.

At the beginning of the ceremony, adult members of the community gather around and observe the shaman sitting in meditative silence. Soon, feeling surrounded by spirit helpers, the shaman declares that 'the way is open' to undertake the journey. Various people then sing in chorus while the shaman undertakes the difficult task of carefully avoiding three large, rolling stones on the sea floor and slipping nimbly past the goddess's snarling watchdog. Rasmussen gives some idea of the perceptual process experienced by the shaman during spirit projection:

He almost glides as if falling through a tube so fitted to his body that he can check his progress by pressing against the sides, and need not actually fall down with a rush. This tube is kept open for him by all the souls of his namesakes, until he returns on his way back to Earth.[10]

The shaman now meets the sea goddess, who appears to be almost suffocating from the impurities of the misdeeds enacted by mankind. As the shaman strokes her hair to placate her, the sea goddess communicates in spirit-language, revealing that on this occasion there have been secret miscarriages among the women, and boiled meat has been eaten in breach of taboo. When the shaman returns in due course to the people, this message will be relayed and the offenders sought out to explain their wrongdoing.

❖

ABOVE *Drumming assists the shaman's spirit-journey.*

We can see from this account that the spirit-journey is not undertaken purely as an indulgence. There is always a clear task involved: to counteract sickness, to understand the nature of breached taboos, to recapture a lost or tormented soul, thereby easing the rift between the spirit world and members of the community.

This, essentially, is the role of the shaman: to journey to other worlds and to use revealed knowledge for a positive outcome. In this way the shaman is an intermediary between the gods and humankind.

WHERE IS
SHAMANISM FOUND?

Shamanism is an extraordinarily far-ranging practice, occurring in many different regions of the world. The classical source literature on shamanism focuses especially on Siberia, and the term 'shaman' itself has entered our language, via the Russian, from the Tungusic word saman. *However, forms of shamanism also occur in North and South America, among the Australian Aborigines, in Indonesia, South-East Asia, China, Tibet and Japan.*

OPPOSITE *Lassooing a
reindeer in
Siberia, one of many
regions where shamanism
is practised.*

❖❖

RIGHT *A Native
American shaman
leads his people to a new
settlement.*

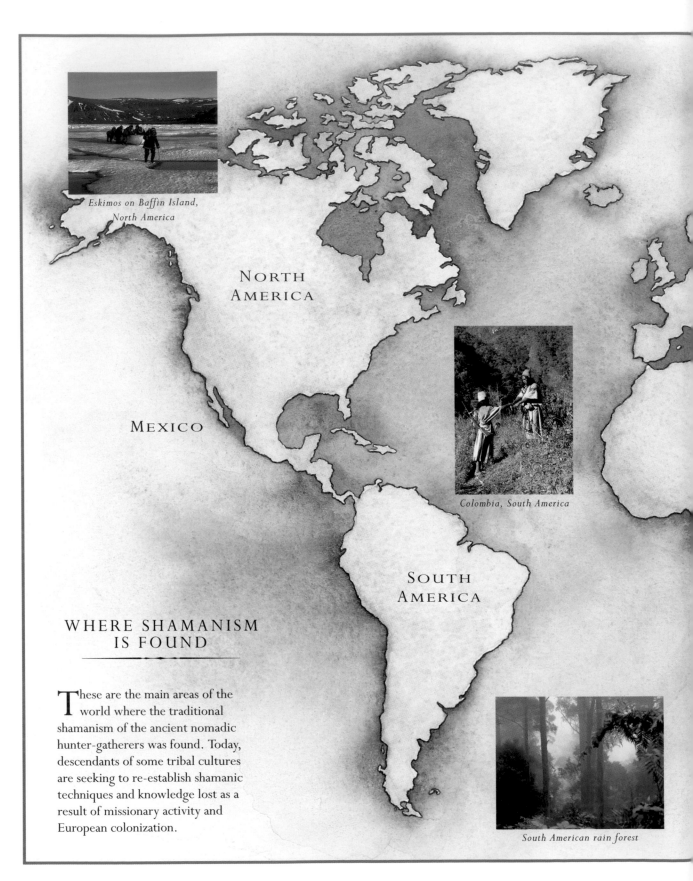

Eskimos on Baffin Island,
North America

NORTH
AMERICA

MEXICO

Colombia, South America

SOUTH
AMERICA

WHERE SHAMANISM
IS FOUND

These are the main areas of the world where the traditional shamanism of the ancient nomadic hunter-gatherers was found. Today, descendants of some tribal cultures are seeking to re-establish shamanic techniques and knowledge lost as a result of missionary activity and European colonization.

South American rain forest

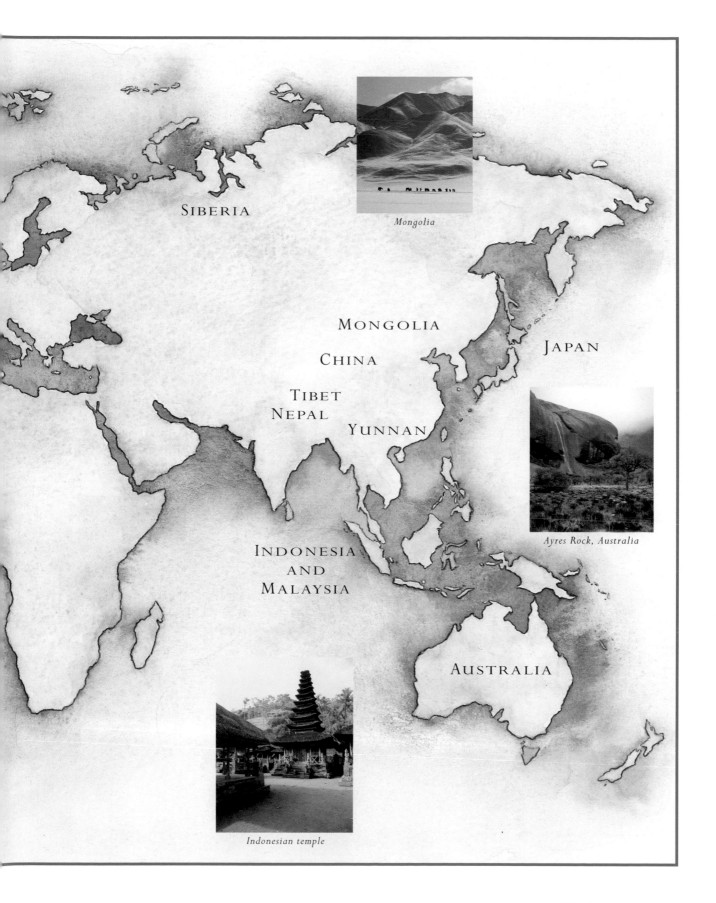

SIBERIA

Mongolia

MONGOLIA

CHINA

JAPAN

TIBET
NEPAL
YUNNAN

Ayres Rock, Australia

INDONESIA
AND
MALAYSIA

AUSTRALIA

Indonesian temple

SIBERIA

This vast region (stretching from the Urals in the west to the Altai Mountains in the south and the Arctic Ocean in the north) encompasses tundra, fertile plains and rugged, mineral-rich mountain systems. It is also the home of many diverse and exotic peoples, including the Buryat and Goldi, the nomadic reindeer-herding Chukchee of the north-east, the Turkic-speaking Kirghiz, Yakuts, Uighurs and Altaians, and the Evenks and other neighbouring tribes in the Tungus-speaking region near the Yenisey and Lena rivers.

The shaman is both a healer and ecstatic who undertakes journeys to the sky and underworld in search of fugitive souls that are responsible for illness. Shamans also utilize divination and clairvoyance, and are sometimes capable of handling fire-coals without being burned.

Buryats distinguish between 'white' shamans who liaise with the gods, and 'black' shamans who summon spirits. Yakuts contrast the gods 'above', regarded as passive and comparatively powerless, with the gods 'below' who have closer ties with the Earth. Yakuts believe they have obtained mastery of fire from Ulu-Toyan, who dwells in the third heaven. This god also created birds, woodland animals and the forests.

The Chukchee believe that spirits may be contacted in dreams and that shamans can utilize them to recover the lost souls of sick patients. The shaman is said to 'open' the patient's skull and replace the soul, which has been captured in the form of a fly or bee.

LEFT *A village in Siberia. Shamanism is widespread amongst the many different peoples who live in this country.*

❖

OPPOSITE *Nomadic peoples carve a living from the spartan environment of the tundra. Shamans may ask the spirits for help in finding food.*

Journey into the Sky

The Altaian shaman sacrifices a horse, addresses the master of fire, fumigates the ritual drum, invokes a multitude of spirits, and then calls to the Markut, the birds of heaven.

After a complex ceremony of purification, the shaman beats the drum violently, indicating a 'mounting' into the sky, accompanied by the spirit of the dead horse. After ascending through several heavens in visionary consciousness, the shaman converses with the creator god Yayutsi and also bows before the Moon and Sun in turn. Finally, at the celestial abode of Bai Ulgan, the shaman learns details of future weather patterns and the outcome of the harvest. The shaman then collapses in a state of ecstatic release.

Bai Ulgan seems to be a god of the 'atmosphere', and it is not uncommon for Indo-European shamans to sacrifice horses to a god of the sky or storms.[1]

The Underworld

Goldi shamans specialize in funerary activities, guiding the deceased into the realms of the underworld. The Goldi shaman calls on spirit helpers for guidance whilst accompanying the dead person, who is mounted on a sled together with food for the journey, toward the land of the departed. The shaman subsequently locates relatives of the deceased, so that the newly departed soul is safely accepted in the underworld. Only then does the Goldi shaman return to the world of the living.

Evenk shamans also accompany the souls of the dead to the underworld, where the deceased then lead a life substantially similar to the life they left behind: they continue to fish and hunt as before, although not visible to mortal eyes. Evenk shamans also use whirlpools to enter the cosmic river, where they encounter the *khargi* spirits of the lower world. The *khargi* are able to assist the shaman in counteracting the effects of evil spirits who are stealing the souls of the living, or causing failures in the hunt.[2]

NORTH AMERICA

BELOW *Shamanic traditions are often interwoven into the practices of other spiritual leaders.*

In North America, shamanism is found among the Tlingit of the north-west coast; the Paviotso hunters, fishers and gatherers from western Nevada; the Mescalero and Chiricahua Apache hunters of Texas, Arizona and New Mexico; the Lakota Sioux of Dakota; also the Nez Perce, Ojibwa (also known as Chippewa), Zuni and Twana.

Shamanic traditions still survive among the Pacific coast Indians such as the Pomo and Salish, the Chumash (who formerly occupied the region around Ojai), and tribes such as the Yurok, Wintu and Karok of north-western California. However, in Native American societies, it has become difficult to distinguish between shamans and other technicians of sacred knowledge: priests, medicine men and women, and sorcerers.

Ghost Dance Religion

The ecstatic movement known as the ghost dance religion, which flourished throughout the 19th century, brought a messianic emphasis to Native American tradition by focusing on the end of the world and the future regeneration of the planet by Indians, both dead and alive. The ghost dance religion did exhibit mystical tendencies – practitioners entered a state of trance and dancers would often become healers – but it differed from traditional shamanism by making it potentially a 'collective' experience for its members.

Dick Mahwee

The Paviotso Dick Mahwee has
described how he obtained his first
shamanic visions during a dream in a
cave near Dayton, when he was 50 years
old. In a state of seemingly 'conscious
sleep', Mahwee had a mystical encounter
with a tall, thin Indian holding an eagle
tail-feather, who taught him ways of
curing sickness. Mahwee utilized trance
states in his shamanizing:

'I smoke before I go into the trance. While I
am in the trance no one makes any noise. I
go out to see what will happen to the
patient. When I see a whirlwind I know that
it caused the sickness. If I see the patient
walking on grass and flowers it means that
he will get well; he will soon be up and
walking. If the flowers are withered or look
as if the frost had killed them, I know that
the patient will die. Sometimes in a trance I
see the patient walking on the ground. If he
leaves footprints I know that he will live, but
if there are no tracks, I cannot cure him.
When I am coming back from the trance, I sing.
I sing louder and louder until I am completely
conscious. Then the men lift me to my feet and I
go on with the doctoring.'[3]

Dreams

The Yurok, Wintu and Karok Indians pay
special regard to their dreams for signs of
omens, portents and psychic attack. For
example, the appearance of an owl in a dream
could be a sign that an evil shaman is
endeavouring to cause harm. This would
cause considerable stress and often ensuing
sickness to the dreamer.

Sometimes a hostile 'force' is also conveyed
by an *uma'a*: a type of psychic arrow fired at
night towards the victim. A shaman-healer is
then required to suck the arrows out of the
victim's body to effect a healing.

Apache Indians

Apache Indians express a strong fear of the
dead, especially dead relatives; also of illnesses
resulting from contact with certain animals,
such as bears and snakes. They also fear owls
because they believe that ghosts appear in this
form. Illness resulting from persecution by
ghosts is referred to as either 'ghost sickness',
'owl sickness' or 'darkness sickness'.

The Apache fearing attack of this kind may
utilize the powers of a shaman-healer who
'sings' over the patient to determine the
nature of the bewitchment.[3]

ABOVE *A shaman*
gathers herbs to use for a
healing ceremony.

❖

LEFT *Charm for use in a*
ritual dance. The owl
represents the soul of a
deceased person.

MEXICO

OPPOSITE *Many
hallucinogenic plants
grow in Mexico. These
form an important part
of local shamanic
culture.*

❖

ABOVE *Pilgrims
may travel hundreds
of kilometres to reach
sacred peyote regions.*

Mexico is home to many shamanic cultures. Since this part of the world is especially rich in hallucinogenic plants, there tends to be a high incidence of psychedelic shamanism. Examples include the Yaquis of northern Mexico, who ritually smoke the yellow *Genista canariensis* flower containing cytisine, and the Huichols, who conduct peyote pilgrimages in sacred parts of the north-central Mexican desert. Also part of this psychedelic tradition are the Tarahumara Indians of Chihuahua, who sometimes add *Datura inoxia* to the fermented maize drink *tesguino*.

A number of Mexican Indian tribes also consume sacred mushrooms as part of their vision quest. These include the Mazatecs, Chinantecs, Zapotecs, and Mixtecs, all of whom come from Oaxaca.

The subject of shamanism and the use of sacred plants as drugs is covered in depth in Chapter 5.

SOUTH AMERICA

This region is characterized by many exotic healing practices, not all of them shamanic. The distinction between a *curandero* and a shaman is not always clear, and there are also various spiritist traditions which are unrelated to shamanism. For example, the practices of French spiritualist Allan Kardec have been very influential in Brazil, as has Macumba: a magical religion similar to Haitian voodoo, which combines folk superstitions, African animism and aspects of Christianity.

Psychedelic Plants

As in Mexico, shamanism in South America tends to be psychedelic, making frequent use of tropical plants which contain hallucinogenic alkaloids. Banisteriopsis vine is widely utilized by South American shamans in the forests of the upper Amazon. The visions it produces are believed to represent encounters with supernatural forces. The Jivaro of Ecuador, the Shipibo-Conibo, Campa, Sharanahua and Cashinahua of eastern Peru, and the Sione Indians of eastern Colombia use this plant.

The celebrated Eduardo Calderón, a Peruvian artist and shaman, used the hallucinogenic San Pedro cactus, which has been in continuous use in Peruvian shamanism for an estimated 3,000 years. Calderón was something of a special case, combining shamanic trance visions with prayers and invocations to Jesus Christ, the Virgin Mary and other important figures from the Christian tradition.

OPPOSITE *Colombia: home to the Sione Indians, who encounter supernatural forces through the use of hallucinogens.*

❖

❖

BELOW *The Amazon. Shamans living among the tribes in the rain forests of the Amazon use the banisteriopsis plant.*

Dreamtime pictures are used in the aboriginal culture to record dream journeys.

AUSTRALIA

Aborigines

Among Australian Aborigines, the shaman or medicine man is known as a *karadji*, or 'clever man'. Aboriginal culture extends back at least 40,000 years. Today the principal regions where traditional Aboriginal religion is still found are Arnhem Land, in central northern Australia, and the central Australian desert. There are scattered communities in other regions.

Magic

Aborigines believe illness, death and accidents are caused by magic or animistic actions. The shaman operates in a world where both imitative and contagious magic are practised.

In imitative magic, the anticipated result is imitated in ritual. For example, the image of a person may be subjected to hostile acts (pins, burning etc).

In contagious magic, objects which have been in contact with each other are believed to be linked. This link permits magic to be used to cause harm, for example by a rite performed over fingernails, hair clippings or possessions.

Aboriginal magicians may also 'sing' a person to death or 'point the bone' (a type of projective magic where a kangaroo bone or carefully prepared stick is pointed at the intended victim).

Initiation

The shamanic aspect of Aboriginal culture is evident in the initiation of medicine men. Among the Arunta and Aranda, the candidate goes to the mouth of a particular cave where he is 'noticed' by the spirits of the dreamtime. They throw an invisible lance at him, which pierces his neck and tongue, and another which passes through his head from ear to ear. Dropping down 'dead', he is carried by the spirits into the cave and his internal organs replaced with new ones, together with a supply of magical quartz crystals upon which his 'power' will later depend.

When he rejoins his people as a person 'reborn', he has a new status as a shaman-healer, although he will not normally perform as a *karadji* for a year or so.

Baiame

The power of the crystals stems from the fact that they are believed to embody the essence of Baiame, the all-father or great sky god.

For the Wiradjeri Aborigines, Baiame is a very old man, with a long beard, sitting in his camp. Two huge quartz crystals extend from his shoulders to the sky above him.

Baiame may bestow shamanic abilities on Aborigines through their dreams. He causes a sacred waterfall of liquid quartz to pour over the dreamer's body, absorbing him totally. He grows wings, replacing his arms, and learns to fly. Baiame sinks a piece of magical quartz into the dreamer's forehead, bestowing the ability to see inside physical objects. An inner flame and an invisible cord of flame are also incorporated into the body of this new shaman. This provides a link with Baiame and enables the shaman to travel up into the sky.

Shamanic Practices

Aboriginal shamans may learn of magical portents through dreams. Initiates also appear to use out-of-the-body states to perceive events at a distance.[5]

Bull-roarers may be used by shamans to produce an altered state of consciousness which can be utilized magically. The bull-roarer is swung around in the air, producing a unique sound, which is said to be the voice of Baiame. Those present stare into a fire in the middle of the sacred circle, where visions begin to appear in the flames. *Karadijis* are said to be able to roll in the fire and scatter hot coals without being burned.

These beliefs and practices have all the hallmarks of classic shamanism.

INDONESIA AND MALAYSIA

Tupa-Jing

Dyaks also refer in their legends to shamanic journeys to the sky. The god Tupa-Jing noticed that the Dyaks were on the verge of extinction because they had no remedies for sickness. So he saved a woman from the funeral pyre, took her to heaven and instructed her in medical skills. Then she was able to return to Earth and pass on the precious knowledge she had obtained.

Notions of spirits and sickness also parallel those found in other shamanic cultures. The Sumatran Kubu believe that sickness arises when a person's soul is captured by a ghost. Shamans, known here as *malims*, are called in to effect an exorcism. During the seance the *malims* dance, fall into a trance, and the chief *malim* is then able to 'see' the patient's soul and retrieve it.

The Underworld

ABOVE *Sumatran tribesman with bow, arrows and* parang *knife.*

❖

RIGHT *Trance states may be used to journey to the underworld.*

Shamans here exhibit many characteristics found elsewhere in the world, including trance states, magical flight and contacts with spirits.

Menangkabau shamans seek visions by travelling deep into the jungle or to the top of high mountains, where they await visitation from the spirits. Iban shamans fast, sleep near a grave or travel to the top of a mountain to obtain magical powers from a guardian spirit. The Iban also refer to the initiation of shamans through a metaphysical 'restructuring' process, which has strong parallels with Aboriginal initiation.

There are also instances where shamans journey to the underworld. During a *belian*, or curing ceremony, a Dyak *manang*, or shaman-healer, falls into a trance state and journeys to the underworld to retrieve the patient's soul, which has been captured by a spirit. Sometimes the *manang* has to lure the evil demon back to the patient's house and kill it.

Among the Karo Bataks, when someone dies, a female shaman dances herself into a state of ecstasy and then explains to the dead person's soul that it has passed through the process of death. At a later ceremony, she then sends the soul off to the land of the dead.[6]

EASTERN ASIA AND THE ORIENT

Here shamanism and animism pre-date the more familiar mainstream religious philosophies such as Buddhism and Confucianism.

Tibet

In Tibet, Bon shamans speak of a sacred rope which in times past linked priests with the celestial dwelling of the gods. Today they are still believed to use their drums to 'propel' themselves through the air.

As with other forms of shamanism, healers here similarly undertake a search for a patient's soul, if its capture (by a spirit) is perceived to be a cause of sickness.

Yunnan

The Lolo of southern Yunnan also believe that in earlier times, people moved more freely between heaven and Earth.

A Lolo shaman-priest officiates in funerary rituals, 'opening the bridge to heaven' and helps the deceased find their way across various mountains and rivers to the Tree of Thought and other regions of the afterlife.

Influenced by Chinese magic, the shamans of Yunnan also practise divination, and undertake visionary journeys on horseback to retrieve lost souls.

China

In China, when Confucianism was established as the State religion in the first century, ecstatics, shamans and diviners were banished, and some were killed. However, some shamanic vestiges remain in the Taoist tradition, which is still served by monasteries and temples throughout the country. Ch'u state, in particular, has been a stronghold of Chinese shamanism.

The most obvious link between Taoism and shamanism is found in meditative practices. Taoists use incense to carry their prayers to heaven, strike pieces of wood together in a monotonous rhythm rather like Siberian shamans with their drums, and believe that they can discover a spirit guide in the 'cave' of the heart. As meditative states become heightened through increasing skills of visualization and breath control, the Taoist then journeys with a spirit guide to distant mystic realms, perhaps communicating with the gods who live in the stars. In so doing, a Taoist meditator is behaving exactly like a shaman.[7]

ABOVE *A South Korean shaman presides at the funeral of a village elder.*

❖

LEFT *A shaman from the Meo tribe in Laos undertakes a ritual.*

Nepal

According to Larry G. Peters, the Tamangs of Nepal also practise an authentic form of shamanism which, though drawing on elements of Hinduism and Buddhism, appears to pre-date them as a spiritual tradition. Peters' key informant, Bhirendra, was the son of a *bombo*, or shaman, who at the age of 13 experienced a spontaneous state of demonic possession which led to his initiatory calling.

Under the guidance of his father, and also the spirit of his deceased grandfather, Bhirendra learned to enter trance states voluntarily and in due course to achieve magical, out-of-the-body flight. Bhirendra described to Peters a vision in which he journeyed to the highest heaven to meet the supreme shaman deity, Ghesar Gyalpo:

❖

'I walked into a beautiful garden with flowers of many different colours. There was also a pond and golden glimmery trees. Next to the pond was a very tall building which reached up into the sky. It had a golden staircase of nine steps leading to the top. I climbed the nine steps and saw Ghesar Gyalpo at the top, sitting on his white throne which was covered with soul flowers. He was dressed in white and his face was all white. He had long hair and a white crown. He gave me milk to drink and told me that I would attain much shakti to be used for the good of my people.'[8]

❖

ABOVE RIGHT *Vestiges of the shamanic tradition are still retained in Nepalese festivals to this day.*

❖

RIGHT *The present-day religions of Japan have incorporated ancient beliefs: the red flower* Houzuki, *for example, is a traditional good-luck symbol of spring.*

Deguchi Onisaburo

Japan

Shamanism is also found in isolated regions of Japan, which is not surprising since it seems likely that Tungusic and Altaic-speaking tribes exerted a cultural influence on Japan prior to the advent of Buddhism, in the third or fourth century.

Female shamans, or *miko* (more common than male shamans) are still found in small villages where they utilize trance, telepathy, mediumism and fortune-telling, and communicate with guardian deities or spirits of the dead. In the larger cities, however, the role of the *miko* has been absorbed by Shinto ritual.

However, it is clear that shamanic episodes can still occur in modern times, as evidenced by the remarkable case of Deguchi Onisaburo, which gave rise to the Omoto religious movement in Japan.

Deguchi Onisaburo

In 1898, Deguchi, who was by all accounts a frail youth, was beaten up by some gamblers and nearly died. He sank into a comatose sleep and on recovering consciousness, declared that he had journeyed to a cave on Mount Takakura. After fasting there, he had travelled through regions of heaven and hell. On his journey he had been granted occult powers of clairvoyance and clairaudience, and had seen as far back as the creation of the world. His visionary experiences included a meeting with the king of the underworld: a creature who in a moment was able to transform from a white-haired old man with a gentle face into a frightening demonic monarch with a bright red face, eyes like mirrors and a tongue of flame.

Deguchi was subsequently 'killed, split in half with a sharp blade like a pear, dashed to pieces on rocks, frozen, burnt, engulfed in avalanches of snow [and] turned into a goddess' and yet, despite all these bizarre occurrences he then found himself at the centre of the world, at the summit of the huge axial mountain Sumeru. Here he was granted a vision of the river leading towards paradise. Before him, on a vast lotus, stood a marvellous palace of gold, agate and jewels. All around were blue mountains and the golden lapping waves of a lake, and golden doves flew above him in the air.[9]

Somewhat unfortunately, Deguchi's experiences led to messianic claims. During World War One he proclaimed that he was an incarnation of Maitreya (the future Buddha destined to descend from Tusita heaven to save the human race) and he also advocated a form of spiritual healing which involved meditative union with the gods.

Deguchi's writings extended to over 80 volumes. His sect is still in existence, even though Deguchi died in 1948 at the age of 78.

3

SHAMANIC COSMOLOGIES

*M*ythologies, cultural heroes and deities differ around the world, and
the relationship between the gods and mankind is perceived in
different ways. Some people view their gods as tyrannical overlords, others as
helpful parental overseers, and some view their deities as supernatural beings
whose power can be usurped with appropriate chants or invocations.

Images

As Eliade notes, different cultures employ
different metaphors and symbols to describe
the zones of the universe. The Turko-Tatars
view the sky as a tent, with the stars as 'holes'
for light, while the Yakuts describe stars as
'windows of the world'. The Pole Star is often
considered to be the centre of the celestial
vault and is variously labelled as Sky Nail by
the Samoyed, the Golden Pillar by the
Mongols and Buryats, and the Iron Pillar by
the Kirghiz.[1]

In societies where there is no symbolic
pillar or axis reaching to heaven, there are
other variants such as cosmic mountains,
ziggurats, temples, palaces, bridges, stairs,
ladders and rainbows or, as with the Evenks,
a mighty river which joins the three levels of
the cosmos. Always, the shaman has some
means of ascending to the cosmic skies or
journeying to the underworld.

The Universe

Despite these differences, when we eliminate
cultural variables there seems to be a remarkable
consensus in shamanic societies about how the
universe is structured. As Mircea Eliade has
indicated in his important work *Shamanism:
Archaic Techniques of Ecstasy* (which has
influenced virtually all shamanic research
since its first publication), the shaman's
universe consists basically of three levels.

Man lives on the Earth in a middle world,
between an upper world and a lower world
(the latter two are often associated
respectively with the sky and underworld).
The three zones are usually linked by a central
vertical axis, which is sometimes referred to
as the *Axis Mundi*, or Axis of the World, and
which is characterized in different
mythologies as the World Tree, the Tree of
Life and so on. This central axis passes
upwards and downwards through 'holes' in
the cosmic vault which lead to the upper and
lower worlds, and it is through these that the
shaman is able to pass from one level of
existence to another, and back again.

ABOVE *The Buddha
stepped on Mount Meru,
the 'centre of the world',
to help him reach
heaven.*

❖❖

RIGHT *Lapp societies
believe in a World
Pillar: two high stones
and a squared log
of wood.*

❖❖

OPPOSITE *The roof
of this Indonesian
temple represents the
cosmic heavenly
mountain, Meru.*

LINKS BETWEEN HEAVEN AND EARTH

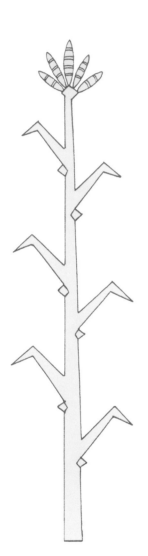

ABOVE *This Navajo Indian Tree of Life is also a corn plant, an important source of food.*

❖❖

RIGHT *Yggdrasil, the World Tree of Norse mythology.*

World Trees

World Trees are quite common in the religions of Central and Northern Asia. The Yakuts of Siberia believe a tree with eight branches rises from the 'golden navel of the Earth' and reaches up to heaven. The first man was born here, and was suckled by a woman who half emerged from the trunk. The Goldi and Dolgan, meanwhile, believe that prior to being born, the souls of little children sit like birds on the branches of the World Tree, and that shamans go there to find them.[2]

The World Tree is also a feature of Norse mythology: Yggdrasil was the sacred ash tree which overshadowed the entire universe, its roots, branches and trunk uniting heaven, Earth and the underworld. According to Norse cosmology, the roots of Yggdrasil lay in the underworld, while the trunk ascended through Midgard, the Earth. Rising through the mountain known as Asgard, the sacred tree branched high into the sky; its leaves were clouds in the sky, and its fruits the stars.

The World Tree also features in Dyak mythology, where it has seven branches and provides a 'road to the sky' for the spirits of the dead, and in like fashion Indonesian shamans climb it to retrieve the lost souls of patients.

Tree of Life

The Osmanli Turks talk of a Tree of Life which has a million leaves, each one containing a human fate. Every time a person dies, a leaf falls.[3]

The Tree of Life is also a central theme in the Jewish mystical kabbalah tradition. It is a complex symbol describing the levels of existence between the transcendent hidden god in Ain Soph Aur (the Limitless Light) and the ten lower sephiroth or spheres of being, which reflect aspects of God's divine nature in the manifested world of creation. For the kabbalist, as for the shaman, the essential mystical purpose is to know God.

Although the animistic frameworks of shamanism are less ethereal and more pragmatic than the quest of the devotional Jewish mystic, it is worth noting that the kabbalistic Tree of Life has also provided a practical focus for modern Western magic, which is in one sense a type of contemporary shamanism.

Mountains and Rivers

Cosmic mountains are found in Indian mythology (Mount Meru being considered the 'centre of the world') and also feature in the legends of ancient Mesopotamia and other regions of the Middle East.

A classic example of a river system offering a link between the three worlds is provided by the religious framework of the Evenks, whose cosmology is characteristic of the Tungus-Manchu peoples of Siberia.

ABOVE *North American Navajo Indian sand paintings from the mountain chant. Used for healing, each painting is 'sung' before being rubbed out and replaced by another.*

LEFT *A diagram of the Tree of Life as viewed by the Jewish kabbalists.*

EVENK COSMOLOGY: *A Special Case*

BELOW *Using an
eagle for hunting. The
clan mistress must be
appeased to ensure a
successful hunt.*

❖

BELOW RIGHT *Birds,
animals and fish are
under the control of
the god Eksheri.*

The Evenks conceive of a universe consisting of the three characteristic levels identified by Eliade. There is an upper world called *ugu buga*, associated with the sky; a middle world called *dulugu buga*, where mankind dwells; and a lower world named *khergu-ergu buga*, which is the domain of deceased kinsmen and the spirits of illness. Linking the three worlds, and providing the counterpart of the cosmic tree, is the mythical Clan river. This originates in the upper world, and flows through to an underground sea extending to the furthest reaches of the lower world.[4]

The Upper World

The upper world, *ugu buga*, to all intents and purposes resembles the familiar world of everyday reality, but on a grander scale. The gods and spirits who dwell here are prototypes for Man below.

Ugu buga is the realm of the creator god Amaka, a very old man dressed in luxuriant fur clothing. In earliest times, Amaka taught humans how to use fire and tools, and how to domesticate reindeer.

Ugu buga is also the dwelling place of Eksheri, considered the master of animals, birds and fish. Eksheri holds the 'threads' of their destiny in his hands, dictating when they live and die. Shamans appeal to Eksheri about the success of the hunt, for if Eksheri is not propitiated, he can direct his spirit rulers to drive the animals away in different directions. Eksheri also represents the 'heavenly' counterpart of the clan mistress of the lower world, the guardian of animal souls sought for the hunt.

Also residing in *ugu buga* is the thunder god Agdy, who upon awakening, gives vent to peals of thunder and flashes of lightning, which destroy evil spirits. Here too lives the old man Dylacha, who, as the master of heat and light, toils unceasingly to provide warmth for mankind: an effort very much appreciated during the Siberian winter. Dylacha lights the heavenly fire, collects its heat in his huge leather bag and then, when the spring comes, dispenses it to the middle world with the assistance of his sons, helping to warm the land and melt the icy rivers.

The Lower World

The beings of the upper world, as one would expect, are considered benevolent, but the dwellers of the lower world are much more formidable.

In the lower world, *khergu-ergu buga*, what has been living becomes dead, and what was dead becomes alive. It is a domain that on one particular level, called *buni*, is inhabited by dead clansmen whose bodies are cold and who live there without breathing, but who nevertheless continue to hunt and fish like the living. *Khergu-ergu buga* is also the realm of the spirits of illness and disease, and of the clan mistress, who watches for breaches of tribal taboos.

The rulers of the lower world, known collectively as the *khargi*, cannot be ignored, for they govern the ancestor spirits and must be respected as overlords of the dead. The Evenks say that the *khargi*, including the clan mistress, are half-animal and half-human, so ironically, despite the dangers, the lower world provides the possibility for totemic clan unity. Shamans are special because they have a sacred link with the totem animal, can conquer the domain of death, and are then 'reborn', alive, into the familiar middle world.

Main

The unique role of the shaman is sometimes represented in hero myths. The Evenks have a legend about a shaman called Main, who is a master of destiny, a hunter in the heavens, and an archetypal cosmic shaman:

One day Kheglen, the heavenly elk, stole the Sun from the sky by impaling it on its antlers. This plunged the world into seemingly eternal night, and humankind was at a loss as to what to do. Main, the hero shaman, then came forth, donned his skis and headed off to the opening in the heavenly vault. Once in *ugu buga*, Main was able to track down the elk and strike it with an arrow from his bow. He thus was able to return the Sun – and all its light and warmth – to the middle world, and in turn became recognized as a guardian of life itself.

A Meeting with the Clan Mistress

Shamans have to negotiate with the clan mistress, Bugady-eninintyn, who dwells in the lower world. She is the guardian of animal souls, and is consulted about the hunt.

Having announced in a song that he will confirm how many animals can be caught in the hunt, the shaman journeys through a whirlpool and along a river to the subterranean clan territories, overcomes various obstacles in his path, and meets the clan mistress face to face.

She appears before him in a forbidding form that is half-animal and half-human. Undaunted by her appearance, he knows he must persuade her to release the animal souls under her command. After pleading with her at length, he is finally granted permission to capture a certain number of animals, which he turns into silken threads and hides inside his drum. When he returns to the middle world, he takes his drum to the clan's hunting grounds and shakes the threads out. These transform into real animals which will provide the future catch for his fellow hunters.

Nevertheless, if appeasing the gods of both the upper and lower worlds is the central task, the shaman does not always act alone. Often accompanied by helper guides, who assist in the passage from one realm to the next, the shaman also invariably has various allies – spirits or familiars – which can help in performing tasks successfully.

ABOVE *Eskimo carving of a shaman and spirit helpers. The drum used to conjure spirits lies alongside.*

❖

SPIRIT GUIDES

In the shaman's world, spirit allies have many functions: they can detect the origins of illness, be despatched to recover lost souls, be summoned in acts of aggression, and show a clear path past obstacles which might arise on the shaman's quest. As we have already seen, spirit guides may appear to shamans in dreams, in visions, and spontaneously after initiations. In some societies, shamans also exchange or inherit spirit guides. In all cases, however, spirit guides are perceived as crucial to the shaman's resolve and power: a literal embodiment of psychic and magical strength.

Types of Spirit Guide

There are two basic types of spirit guide. Firstly, there are spirits which are substantially under the shaman's control and which serve as familiars. But there are also other spirits, thought of more as guardians or helpers, who are available when the shaman needs to call on their aid. These may be minor deities, or the spirits of deceased shamans: entities who maintain a certain independence in their particular realm and who are not automatically subject to the control of the shaman.

Familiars

Siberian shamans generally have animal familiars such as bears, wolves and hares, or birds such as geese, eagles or owls. Yakuts, for example, view bulls, eagles and bears as their strongest allies, preferring them to wolves or dogs (the spirits of lesser shamans). The Barama Carib, meanwhile, associate different classes of spirit with different types of pebble which are placed in the shaman's rattle. These spirits can be summoned at will.

Guardians and Helpers

The guardian spirit, or spirit helper, is on a different level. The example in Chapter 2, of Tamang shamanism in Nepal, provides this distinction. Here Bhirendra was guided by the spirit of his dead grandfather, and it was through him, as well as through the tutelage of his father, that he was able to acquire shamanic visionary consciousness.

Sometimes, as Mircea Eliade has pointed out, the guardian spirit also becomes a type of alter ego of the shaman: a psychic counterpart on the inner planes. To this extent, we can understand the magical claims of human-animal transformation. On these occasions, the shaman projects consciousness into an animal form on an imaginal level. It is in this 'body' that the shaman goes forth on the spirit-journey.

Chukchee and Eskimo shamans maintain that they can change themselves into wolves, while Lapps can become bears or reindeers. The Semang shamans of the Malay Peninsula, on the other hand, believe they can transform themselves into tigers. This type of magical transformation is not without its dangers, however. Sometimes shamans fight each other on the inner planes in their magical bodies. If a shaman 'dies' during this encounter, it is often said that death will result in real life as well, for the shaman's 'essence' will have been destroyed.

LEFT *An 1840 Tlingit screen from Alaska, depicting the clan crest of a bear.*

❖

OPPOSITE *A Huron boy on a vision quest is protected by the spirit of a wolf.*

Netsilik Shamans

On the more basic level of animal familiars, a good example of their role is provided by the Netsilik Eskimos of the Arctic coast of Canada. Here established shamans, or *angatkoks*, recruit prospective young male shamans and put them through a magical apprenticeship. They join the household of a shaman-teacher, are instructed in observing ritual taboos, and then move to a special igloo where they learn shamanic techniques. The teacher provides his novice with a *tunraq* (a spirit helper or familiar), and in the beginning it is clear that the *tunraq* has more power than its new owner. However, with time the young shaman learns to tame it. As the shaman grows in experience and confidence, he may later acquire further *tunraqs* and can keep doing so throughout his life.

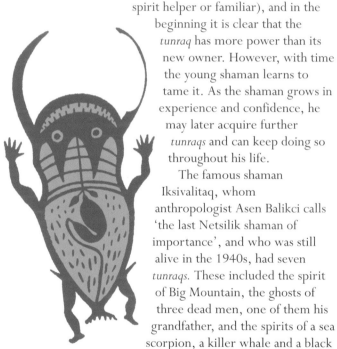

The famous shaman Iksivalitaq, whom anthropologist Asen Balikci calls 'the last Netsilik shaman of importance', and who was still alive in the 1940s, had seven *tunraqs*. These included the spirit of Big Mountain, the ghosts of three dead men, one of them his grandfather, and the spirits of a sea scorpion, a killer whale and a black dog without ears.

According to Asen Balikci, who studied Netsilik culture in some detail, *tunraqs* like to be 'frequently called and used', thus reinforcing the notion that ideally there should be a strong personal bond between shamans and their spirit guides. But it is also possible for *tunraqs* to unleash their potency against their owners if things go wrong. Perhaps a shaman has sent the *tunraq* on a difficult mission and the spirit has failed to achieve its task. It can then become a 'reversed spirit' or *tunraq kigdloretto*: angry, bloodthirsty and out of control, wreaking havoc on its former owner and relatives, and bringing sickness and death.

Tunraq Stories

Even at the best of times, in Netsilik society *tunraqs* have an uneasy relationship with their irascible owners. Balikci quotes two cases where aggressive shamanizing was the result of jealous rivalry:

Kaormik was a better bear hunter than Amaoligardjuk's son, so Amaoligardjuk, a shaman, became jealous and sent his tunraq polar bear against Kaormik. The bear scratched the left side of his face severely but failed to kill him. Amaoligardjuk added: 'This man is hard to kill!'

And on another occasion:

Tavoq, a shaman, grew jealous of Angutitak, an excellent hunter, and scolded him repeatedly. Angutitak, a quiet and fearful man, never answered, until one day he accused Tavoq of being a mediocre and lazy hunter. Tavoq avenged himself by despatching his tunraq to raise a snowstorm just at the moment when Angutitak was stalking caribou. [5]

Goldi Shamans

Another remarkable instance of the sometimes precarious relationship between a shaman and his or her spirit guide, is provided by an unnamed Goldi shaman who had lengthy discussions with Russian anthropologist Lev Shternberg in the early 1900s. He explained to Shternberg that he had initially been drawn to shamanism after suffering bad headaches. Other shamans were unable to cure him, and so he yearned to be a shaman himself.

One night while he was asleep on his bed, he was visited by a female spirit. She resembled a Goldi woman but was much smaller (around 70cm in height). She told him that she was an *ayami* (one of his ancestor spirits), and had taught shamanic healing to other shamans. Now she was going to teach him.

The *ayami* also said that she would now regard the man as her husband and would provide him with spirit familiars to assist him in healing. She was also somewhat threatening. 'If you will not obey,' she told him sternly, 'so much the worse for you. I shall kill you.'[6]

The shaman related to Shternberg how his spirit wife could change form at will, sometimes appearing as an old woman, sometimes as a wolf or winged tiger. She took him on aerial journeys to other locations. She also bequeathed him three familiars – a panther, bear and tiger – to help out during his shamanizing. It was they who provided the source of his shamanic power: 'When I am [shamanizing] the *ayami* and the familiars are possessing me,' he told Shternberg; 'whether big or small, they penetrate me, as smoke or vapour would. When the *ayami* is within me, it is she who speaks through my mouth.'[7]

We see here a blurring of the distinction made earlier between shamans and mediums: in a sense this shaman has become possessed by his spirit guides. However, it is really a case of the shaman consciously tapping his inner resources, in this case his multiple spirit guides, to perform the act of magical healing. To this extent he is still exercising his will, rather than responding passively to the situation, and channelling an unknown force from realms beyond his mind.

Relationship

Overall, the relationship between the shaman and his or her spirit guides is a vital but sometimes precarious one. The spirit guides may, for a time, dictate the state of play.

Sometimes the relationship might take the form of a spiritual 'marriage', as in the case of the Goldi shaman, or else it might involve the shaman honouring spirit helpers through song, dance and ritual. It might entail making offerings to fetishes linked to the spirit guides, actively respecting taboos (for example, not eating the meat of the animal concerned) or simply agreeing to keep the existence of the spirit ally a secret from others.

Whatever the situation, it is clear that in the final analysis shamans depend very much on their spirit guides, whether they are animal familiars under the shamans' control, or cosmic denizens who hold the key to realms beyond, in the upper and lower worlds. A shaman's unique role, after all, is as an intermediary. Shamans are special because they are effective on more than one plane of reality, and it is up to them to maintain that special access by mustering all the assistance they can obtain.

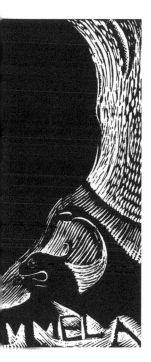

ABOVE *Netsilik shamans may acquire several spirit helpers during their lifetime.*

❖❖

RIGHT *Performing a dance to appease the snake god. Symbolic body painting, such as the snake and beaver shown here, was commonly practised.*

Spirit Stories

ABOVE Pal-rai-yuk,
*a mythical creature resembling
a crocodile.*

❖

RIGHT *The Blackfoot story
of the squaw who married the
morning star, but became
homesick and returned to Earth
as a falling star.*

❖

BELOW *Spirit mask
of the wild dog, wolf
and fox.*

ABOVE *Humming
bird spirits.*

❖

LEFT *Apache Indians
fear owls because they
believe that ghosts
appear in this form.*

LEFT *The Chinook tale of supernatural people descending from the skies to help the destitute children of a chief.*

❖

RIGHT *Animals featuring in Xingu myths, (from top) the agouti, paca and tanandua.*

❖

BELOW LEFT *The Chinook were buried in their canoes, which floated down river to shadowland, where the dead lived.*

❖

BELOW *Mamaés, Amazon Indian spirits of the dead.*

4

RITUALS
AND THE
INNER WORLD

Ceremonial ritual is the outer enactment of an internal event. In all religions, and also in shamanism and ceremonial magic, those performing a ritual believe that what they are doing is not simply theatrical but accords with some sort of sacred, inner reality. For a time they are caught up in a mystical drama, perhaps involving union with a god, identification with a source of spiritual healing or the act of embodying some sort of transcendent power. In such a way the shaman, priest or magician believes that he or she is tapping into a dimension which is much larger and more awesome than the familiar world of reality. It is very much a case of participating in a mystery, of leaving the everyday realm and, for a sacred and special period of time, entering the cosmos.

Zuni Pueblo

American anthropologist Michael Harner describes the transformatory nature of ritual in evaluating the dance of the beast gods as performed by the Zuni Pueblo:

The beast gods are summoned by dancing, rattling and drumming, and the dancers work themselves into a frenzied condition in which they imitate the actions and cries of animals. Those dancers assuming the personality of the bear may even wear actual bear paws over their hands. But this dance of the beast gods is more than simple imitation, since the Zuni dancer, like the North American Plains Indian doing an eagle or buffalo dance, is striving to go beyond imitation to become one with the animal … Likewise, a Zuni dancer wearing the mask of one of the kachina *gods is doing more than impersonating the* kachina. *Transported into an altered state of consciousness by the dancing, drumming, rattling and whirr of bull-roarers, he 'becomes for the time being the actual embodiment of the spirit which is believed to reside in the mask'.*[1]

Aborigines

Another example is provided by the Australian Aborigines of Forrest River, who undertake ceremonial initiations which feature the symbolic death and resurrection of the candidate and his ascent to the sky:

The usual method is as follows. The master assumes the form of a skeleton and equips himself with a small bag, in which he puts the candidate, whom his magic has reduced to the size of an infant. Then seating himself astride the rainbow-serpent, he begins to pull himself up by his arms, as if climbing a rope. When near the top, he throws the candidate into the sky, 'killing' him. Once they are in the sky, the master inserts into the candidate's body small rainbow-serpents, brimures [small freshwater snakes], and quartz crystals (which have the same name as the mythical rainbow-serpent). After this operation the candidate is brought back to Earth, still on the rainbow-serpent's back. The master again introduces magical objects into his body, this time through the navel, and wakens him by touching him with a magical stone. The candidate returns to normal size. On the following day the ascent by the rainbow serpent is repeated in the same way.[2]

ABOVE *Aranda Aborigine men carefully apply symbolic decorative body paint.*

RIGHT *Performing a buffalo dance, in which the dancers take on the personality of the animal.*

OPPOSITE *The tribe gathers round as the shaman executes a medicine pipe stem dance.*

Reality and Magic

Clearly, in such rituals there are physical observances (that one can actually see) and symbolic, mythic processes that are represented by the ceremonial sequence of events. Unlike the scientifically trained Western observer, who no doubt would miss much of the import of a ritual such as the Aboriginal one described, the shaman does not distinguish between 'real' and 'unreal' worlds. The entire magical domain explored during the shamanizing is an integrated expression of both 'natural' and 'magical' events, for the shaman is 'breaking through in plane' from everyday reality to the upper or lower worlds. For the shaman, in a nutshell, the magic is real.

ABOVE *A ceremonial drum of the American Pawnee Indians.*

❖

RIGHT *This Mongolian shaman's costume is decorated with metal objects and bells.*

Costume

When we look at shamanic costumes, we can see evidence of the mythic processes involved in shamanism. The Japanese shamans observed by Carmen Blacker wore caps of eagle and owl feathers, and cloaks adorned with stuffed snakes, intended to facilitate 'the passage from one world to another'. Emphasizing this point, Blacker notes that 'the magic clothes and instruments, of which the drum is the most important, embody in their shape, in the materials of which they are made, in the patterns and figures engraved upon them, symbolic links with the other world.'[3]

Likewise, Yakut shamans wear a kaftan decorated with a solar disc (representing the opening of the underworld), while Goldi shamans don a coat depicting the cosmic tree and 'power animals' such as bears and wildcats, which are part of their mythic experience. Teleut shamans often wear winged owl caps to symbolize magical flight, while the Buryat shaman costume is heavily laden with iron ornaments portraying the iron bones of immortality. The bears, leopards, serpents and lizards which appear on it are the shaman's spirit helpers.

The Shaman's Universe

To some extent, then, one is obliged to heed the shaman's own perceptions of the universe. For many anthropologists, especially those not attuned to the mind-set of the shaman, this is especially difficult. However, the apparently formidable gap between scientific anthropology and mythic experiential shamanism is capable of being narrowed.

More psychologists are now taking note of such phenomena as near-death and out-of-the-body experiences which strongly suggest that consciousness can operate functionally at a distance from the body. In these experiences, ordinary citizens in an urban Western environment have reported aerial sensations not so far removed from the shamanic experience. The following descriptions from the Winnebago shaman, Thunder Cloud, are much more believable than they first seem, when considered in this context.

Thunder Cloud

Thunder Cloud was a member of the medicine dance secret society and a highly respected shaman. He maintained that he was able to consciously recall two previous incarnations. In the second he actually watched the people burying him after his death, and then journeyed towards the setting Sun, arriving at a village where there were other dead people:

I was told that I would have to stop there for four nights, but, in reality, I stayed there for four years. The people enjoy themselves here. They have all sorts of dances of a lively kind. From that place we went up to where Earthmaker lives and I saw him and talked to him, face to face, even as I am talking to you now. I saw the spirits too and, indeed, I was like one of them.
Thence I came to this Earth for the third time and here I am. I am going through the same that I knew before.[4]

One can only conclude that the world of the shaman, bizarre as it must sometimes seem to outsiders, is nevertheless totally real to the person experiencing it. Thunder Cloud also describes shamanic dancing and healing from the view of the spirit-vision associated with it:

At Blue Clay Bank [St Paul] there lives one who is a dancing grizzly-bear spirit. Whenever I was in great trouble, I was to pour tobacco, as much as I thought necessary, and he would help me. This grizzly bear gave me songs and the power of beholding a holy thing: he gave me his claws, claws that are holy. Then the grizzly bear danced and performed while he danced. He tore his abdomen open and, making himself holy, healed himself again. This he repeated. One grizzly bear shot claws at the other and the wounded one became badly choked with blood. Then both made themselves holy again and cured themselves.[5]

Clearly, in this instance Thunder Cloud is speaking both literally and metaphysically. Although the grizzly-bear spirit is associated with a specific location (Blue Clay Bank), the descriptions provided are of magical events. Thunder Cloud has seen the miraculous healing, not on a physical level, but in his spirit-vision. Nevertheless, the two levels of perception have begun to merge. The demonstration of healing has provided what the shaman himself calls 'holy' revelations. The shamanizing is occurring in sacred space.

Technique

Having explored aspects of the shaman's experiential realm we should now also consider two of the specifics of shamanic technique: the shaman's drum and use of song. Both are of central importance, since they offer a means of entering the shamanic state of consciousness and attracting spirit helpers. Without skills of this sort, a shaman can hardly hope to be successful.

ABOVE *Necklace of grizzly-bear claws, worn to show bravery in contact with the bear spirit.*

THE SHAMAN'S DRUM

Transport

The drum has a special role in shamanism, for it is literally the vehicle that 'carries' the shaman to the other world. Often it is closely identified with a horse, or some other sort of animal. Soyots call their drums *khamu-at*, meaning 'shaman horse' and Altaic shamans embellish their drums with horse symbols. Interestingly, the anthropologist L. P. Potapov discovered that the Altaian people name their drums not after the animal whose skin is used in manufacture (camel or dappled horse), but after the domestic horses actually used as steeds. This confirms the idea that the drum is a mode of transport: it is the monotonous rhythm of the drum which the shaman 'rides' into the upper and lower worlds. A Soyot poem also makes this clear:

Skin-covered drum,
Fulfil my wishes,
Like flitting clouds, carry me
Through the lands of dusk
And below the leaden sky,
Sweep along like wind
Over the mountain peaks![6]

The sound of the drum acts as a focusing device. It creates an atmosphere of concentration and resolve, enabling shamans to sink deep into trance as they shift their attention to the inner journey of the spirit.

World Link

It is not uncommon, either, for the drum to have a symbolic link with the centre of the world, or cosmic tree (also known as the World Tree). World Trees provide a link between heaven and Earth.

The Evenks fashion the rims of their drums from the wood of the sacred larch, and Lapp shamans decorate their drums with mythic symbols such as the cosmic tree, the Sun, Moon or rainbow.[7]

Trance States

The two crucial points which emerge are that the shaman's drum not only produces an altered state of consciousness, but confirms the shift in perception (which results from the drumming) as the basis for a mythic encounter.

Recent research among the Salish Indians, undertaken by Wolfgang G. Jilek, found that rhythmic shamanic drumming produces a drumbeat frequency in the theta wave EEG frequency (4–7 cycles/second): the brain wave range associated with dreams, hypnotic imagery and trance.[8] This is hardly surprising, for shamanism is a type of mythic 'lucid dreaming'. In the latter category of dreaming one is 'aware' that one is dreaming and likewise, in shamanism, one is conscious in the altered state and able to act purposefully within it. Shamans invariably report their encounters not as hallucinations or fanciful imagination, but as experientially valid: what happens during the spirit-journey is real in that dimension.

LEFT *A Lapp shaman lies with a drum on his back as he enters a trance.*

ABOVE A *shaman in bear costume brandishes
his drum. The drumbeat assists the shaman in
achieving an altered state of consciousness.*

❖

THE SHAMAN'S SONG

Song is another vital aspect of shamanism. It is through songs and chants that the shaman expresses both power and intent. Songs are the sounds of the gods and spirits and, like the sacred drum, can help the shaman feel propelled by their energy.

Geronimo

The Apache shaman-chief Geronimo once proclaimed:

As I sing, I go through the air to a holy place where Yusun [the Supreme Being] will give me power to do wonderful things. I am surrounded by little clouds, and as I go through the air I change, becoming spirit only.[9]

Magic Songs

The Australian Aborigines also provide an excellent example of the link between musical sounds and the gods. Some Aborigines, for example, believe that their creator gods dwell in bull-roarers. These may be whirled in the air to restore energy and vibrancy to both tribe and totem.

Aborigines also believe that the songs they continue to sing today are the same as those sung by their ancestors in the dreamtime, when the gods brought the world into being. The most sacred songs are chanted at special sites where the gods were thought to roam: these songs are considered to have a special magic which helps to produce abundant food and water supplies.

When the explorers Baldwin Spencer and F. J. Gillen visited the Warraminga Aborigines and neighbouring tribes in 1901, they saw a marvellous fire ceremony where huge torches blazed to the wild music of the *kingilli* singers. They listened to legends about Wollungua, the great serpent whose head reached up to the sky, and when visiting the Kaitish Aborigines, observed a rain-making ceremony which included imitations of the plover call.

OPPOSITE *Ayers Rock in Australia, Aboriginal sacred place.*

LEFT *The famous Apache chief Geronimo (1829–1900), photographed in about 1895.*

BELOW *Warraminga Aborigine men hunting for honey. Warraminga ceremonies were studied by explorers at the beginning of this century.*

Ancestors

The central Australian Ljaba Aranda Aborigines, meanwhile, have a honey-ant song which describes the insects nestling under the roots of mulga trees. But these honey-ants are also thought to be ancestor spirits, with elaborate decorations on their bodies. When the song is sung, the Aborigines performing the ceremony sweep brushes of mulga over themselves, allowing the honey-ant spirits to come forth. At this time, they believe themselves to be magically possessed by the ancestors. Such a song is typical of the sacred music which links Aborigines to the dreamtime of their forefathers.[10]

Song from the Heart

Sometimes, as a bridge to sacred reality, song may also be evoked from the shaman's own being. Anthropologist Joan Halifax writes:

As the World Tree stands at the centre of the vast planes of the cosmos, song stands at the intimate centre of the cosmos of the individual. At that moment when the shaman song emerges, when the sacred breath rises up from the depths of the heart, the centre is found, and the source of all that is divine has been tapped.[11]

ABOVE *The shaman Isaac Tens (second from right) performs a healing ceremony on a patient.*

Isaac Tens' Story

A wonderful description of 'song from the heart' is provided by the North American Gitksan Indian, Isaac Tens. At the age of 30, Tens began to fall into trance states and experienced dramatic, and often terrifying, visions. On one occasion animal spirits and snake-like trees seemed to be chasing him and an owl took hold of him, catching his face and trying to lift him up.

While Tens was on a hunting trip, an owl appeared to him again, high up in a cedar tree. Tens shot the owl and went to retrieve it in the bushes, but found to his amazement that it had disappeared. He then hastened back towards his village, puzzled and alarmed, but on the way again fell into a trance:

When I came to, my head was buried in a snowbank. I got up and walked on the ice up the river to the village. There I met my father who had just come out to look for me, for he had missed me. We went back together to my house. Then my heart started to beat fast, and I began to tremble, just as had happened a while before, when the halaaits [medicine-men] were trying to fix me up. My flesh seemed to be boiling ... my body was quivering. While I remained in this state, I began to sing. A chant was coming out of me without my being able to do anything to stop it. Many things appeared to me presently: huge birds and other animals. They were calling me. I saw a meskyawawderh [a kind of bird] and a mesqagweeuk [bullhead fish]. These were visible only to me, not to the others in my house. Such visions happen when a man is about to become a halaait; they occur of their own accord. The songs force themselves out, complete, without any attempt to compose them. But I learned and memorized these songs by repeating them.[12]

LEFT *Aboriginal animal paintings on a rock. Aborigines believe some creatures are spirits of their ancestors.*

❖❖

A Western Vision

While such visions may seem to belong solely to the exotic world of the primitive shaman, it is interesting that urban Westerners who find themselves in a shamanic context sometimes report comparable initiations. An impressive account is provided by the anthropologist Michael Harner.

In 1959, Harner was invited by the American Museum of Natural History to study the Conibo Indians of the Peruvian Amazon. He set off the following year for the Ucayali river and found the Indians friendly and receptive. Harner, however, wished to be more than an anthropologist: he hoped to be initiated as a shaman.

He was told that to tap the magical reality, he would have to drink the sacred potion *ayahuasca*, made from the banisteriopsis vine. *Ayahuasca* produces out-of-the-body experiences, telepathic and psychic impressions, and spectacular visions. Among the Conibo the sacred drink was also known as 'the little death', and its powers were regarded with awe.

Harner took the shamanic potion at night, accompanied by an elder of the village. Soon the sound of a waterfall filled his ears and his body became numb. As he began to hallucinate he became aware of a giant crocodile, from whose jaws rushed a torrent of water. These waters formed an ocean and Harner saw a dragon-headed ship sailing towards him. Several hundred oars propelled the vessel, producing a rhythmic, swishing sound as it moved along. Harner now experienced the music of the inner worlds:

I became conscious ... of the most beautiful singing I have ever heard in my life, high-pitched and ethereal, emanating from myriad voices on board the galley. As I looked more closely at the deck, I could make out large numbers of people with the heads of blue jays and the bodies of humans, not unlike the bird-headed gods of ancient Egyptian tomb paintings. At the same time, some energy-essence began to float from my chest up into the boat.[13]

Harner's mind now seemed to function on several levels as he was granted sacred visions by the spirit creatures: secrets, they told him, which would normally be given only to those about to die. These visions included a survey of the birth of the Earth, aeons before the advent of Man, and an explanation of how human consciousness had evolved.

In traditional shamanism, irrespective of its cultural context, it is not uncommon for the shaman to be shown by the gods how society came into existence, how the worlds were formed, and how Man has a privileged and special relationship with the gods. What is so interesting about Michael Harner's account is that he was able to enter the shaman's exotic world so totally, despite his Western intellectual background.

OPPOSITE *Pre-Columbian Peruvian textile. Anthropologists discovered an ancient tradition of shamanism amongst Peruvian Indians.*

LEFT *Shaman dressed as an animal performs a ceremonial ritual.*

BELOW LEFT *Michael Harner, who became a shaman while studying the Conibo Indians of the Peruvian Amazon.*

5

SACRED PLANTS

*W̶hereas we in the West perceive drugs invariably as producing a distortion, a
wavering from 'reality', in the prolific world of pre-literate shamanism the exact
opposite is true. The specific varieties of plants, such as mushroom and cacti, which
cause visions and hallucinations, are an essential feature of shamanism in many regions
of the world. Such plants, which are believed to open doors to the heavens, to allow
contact with the gods and spirits, and to permit access to a greater reality
beyond, are regarded as sacred.*

ABOVE *A Kamchatkan
shaman brandishes his
drum. Notice the
ornaments and animal
skins attached to
his robe.*

❖

OPPOSITE *Use of
sacred plants is believed
to allow shamans access
to a reality beyond
everyday life.*

To modern urban Westerners, the idea
of visions induced by psychotropic
means may seem decadent. Indeed, during the
late 1960s, when exploration of psychedelics
was rampant, one would often read in the
press about mystical episodes being 'artificially'
produced by drugs such as LSD and psilocybin.
However for the shamans there is only one
reality: the world of the supernatural.

A revealing anecdote which throws light on
modern attitudes from a shamanic point of
view is provided by anthropologist Peter
Furst, who was present when a newspaper
reporter referred to peyote as a 'drug' in
front of a Huichol shaman. The shaman
replied succinctly: 'Aspirin is a drug,
peyote is sacred.'[1]

Hallucinogens

It is important to be aware, firstly, that
many of the sacred plants used in shamanism
are classed as illegal substances. While by
definition such plants are toxic (and have a
distinct biodynamic effect on the body)
this does not mean that these sacred plants
are invariably poisonous, though some are in
certain dosages.

The plants do not simply modify moods,
but are capable of producing a dramatic and
often profound change in perception. Colours

are enhanced, spirits may materialize – and
perhaps a cosmic bridge or smoke tunnel
appears, allowing the shaman to ascend to
the heavens.

The sacred plants are seen as a doorway to a
wondrous realm, and they are not taken lightly.
The ritual use of hallucinogenic plants is not
recreational, but transformative: shamans
undertake the vision quest to 'learn' to 'see',
not to 'escape' into a world of 'fantasy'.

Hallucinatory States

Psychologists have produced various terms to
describe the substances which produce such
radical shifts in consciousness. Dr Humphry
Osmond, an English psychiatrist, coined the
term *psychedelic,* meaning 'mind-revealing' or
'mind-manifesting'. But a term preferred by
many is *psychotomimetic*: substances which are
capable of inducing temporary psychotic
states of such intensity that the 'visionary' or
'dream' world appears profoundly real.

In shamanic societies, experiences like this
are highly valued. Sacred plants remove the
barriers between humankind and the realm of
gods and spirits, from whom one receives
wisdom and learning. The gods *know*; the
sacred plant *speaks.*

Plant Sites

Generally, the psychotropic components of
sacred plants are contained in the alkaloids,
resins, glucosides and essential oils found in
the leaves, bark, stem, flowers, sap, roots or
seeds of the plants. The regions richest in
naturally occurring hallucinogenic plants are
Mexico and South America.

With the exception of *Amanita muscaria*,
datura and marijuana, Asia is comparatively
lacking in such plant species. Plants do not
appear to be used shamanically to any great
extent in Africa and Australasia.

In Mexico the most important plants are
peyote, psilocybe mushrooms and morning-
glory, while in South America the most
prevalent hallucinogen is a drink made from
the banisteriopsis vine, known variously as
ayahuasca, caapi, or *natemaoryaje.*

PEYOTE

Visionary Cactus

Deriving its name from the Aztec *peyotl*, the famous peyote cactus (*Lophophora williamsii*) was the first hallucinogenic plant discovered by Europeans in the Americas. It is associated primarily with the Huichol Indians of the Sierra Madre in Mexico, although it is also used by the Cora and Tarahumara Indians, the American Kiowa and Comanche, and in the more recently established Native American Church.

Effects

Peyote is a complex hallucinogenic plant capable of producing a wide range of effects. Its main alkaloid constituent is mescaline, but it also contains around 30 other psychoactive agents. Users may experience vividly coloured images, shimmering auras around objects, a feeling of weightlessness, and unusual auditory and tactile sensations.

The first detailed description of the cactus was provided by Dr Francisco Hernandez, physician to King Philip II of Spain, who studied Aztec medicine:

The root is of nearly medium size, sending forth no branches or leaves above the ground, but with a certain woolliness adhering to it on account of which it could not aptly be figured by me. Both men and women are said to be harmed by it. It appears to be of a sweetish taste and moderately hot. Ground up and applied to painful joints, it is said to give relief. Wonderful properties are attributed to this root, if any faith can be given to what is commonly said among them on this point. It causes those devouring it to be able to foresee and predict things.[2]

Not surprisingly, the cactus was fiercely suppressed in Mexico by Christian missionaries because of its 'pagan' associations. The Huichol Indians managed to escape the missionaries' proselytizing, even though the Sierra Madre came under Spanish influence in 1722.

Pilgrimage

Today the Indians continue to regard the peyote cactus as divine, associating the region where it grows with paradise (*wirikuta*) and the plant itself with the divine deer, or master of the deer species.

Each year groups of Huichols make a pilgrimage to gather peyote, which they call *hikuri*. They are led by a shaman who is in contact with Tatewari, the peyote god. Tatewari is the archetypal 'first shaman' who led the first peyote pilgrimage, and subsequent shamans seek to emulate his example.

The distance between the Sierra Madre and the high desert of San Luis Potosi where the cactus grows, is hundreds of kilometres. Although in the past this pilgrimage was always undertaken on foot, it is now considered permissible to travel by car, bus or train providing offerings, prayers and acts of ritual cleansing are made en route. The desert destination, Wirikuta, is regarded as the mythic place of origin of the Huichols.

The divine deer, personified by the sacred cactus of the region, is believed to represent life itself. When the shaman leading the pilgrimage finds the peyote, he declares that he has 'seen the deer tracks'. He then 'shoots' the cactus with his bow and arrow as if it were a deer pursued in the hunt.

The peyote cactus is subsequently collected and shared out to those participating in the pilgrimage. The cactus is either consumed direct in small pieces, or macerated and mixed with water (symbolizing the dry and wet seasons). Huichols say the sacred deer is a mount to the upper levels of the cosmos. It is also a spirit helper who can be called upon during healing ceremonies.

ABOVE *Peyote users may experience a sense of weightlessness.*

PSILOCYBE MUSHROOMS

Investigation

BELOW *A Guatemalan mushroom stone. The powers of sacred mushrooms were held in great awe. Psilocybe mushrooms produce vivid hallucinations and sound effects.*

For a long time, the existence of the 'sacred mushrooms' of Mexico was doubted by expert botanists. In 1915 William Safford addressed the Botanical Society in Washington, arguing that sacred inebriating mushrooms did not exist and had been confused with peyote. It took Richard Evans Schultes, Professor of Natural Sciences at Harvard University and Director of the Harvard Botanical Museum, to correct this mistaken impression.

In 1938, Schultes visited the little town of Huautla de Jimenez in the Sierra Mazateca mountains. He obtained specimens of the sacred mushrooms and returned with them to Harvard. A Protestant missionary and linguist, Eunice V. Pike, who had worked among the Mazatecs, also knew about the mushrooms. It was as a result of her letters, and Schultes' field study articles, that retired banker R. Gordon Wasson and his wife Valentina embarked on their celebrated 'pilgrimage' to experience sacred mushrooms at first hand. Wasson brought the issue to prominence in 1957 with an article in *Life* magazine describing 'the awe and reverence ... of a shamanic mushroom *agape*'.[3]

Effects

The most important of the shamanic mushrooms in Mexico is the species *Psilocybe mexicana*, which grows in wet pasture lands, although other, related types of mushroom are also consumed.

Psilocybe mushrooms provide a state of intoxication characterized by vivid, colourful hallucinations and unusual auditory effects. It is for the latter reason that the Mazatecs say, respectfully, that 'the mushrooms speak'.

Usage

We are extremely fortunate to have a poetic account of native mushroom practices from Henry Munn, who lived for many years among the Mazatecs of Oaxaca, and who married the niece of a shaman couple. Munn's article *The Mushrooms of Language* reveals:

The shamans who eat them, their function is to speak, they are the speakers who chant and sing the truth, they are the oral poets of their people, the doctors of the word, they who tell what is wrong and how to remedy it, the seers and oracles, the ones possessed by the voice.[4]

There is also an intriguing tendency among the Mazatecs to blend folk traditions and mythology with Christian beliefs. According to Munn, the Mazatecs say that:

Through their miraculous mountains of light and rain ... Christ once walked   it is a transformation of the legend of Quetzalcoatl — and from where dropped his blood, the essence of his life, from there the holy mushrooms grew, the awakeners of the spirit, the food of the luminous one.[5]

Mazatec shamans only utilize sacred mushrooms to diagnose disease, contacting the spirits causing illness. If there is nothing wrong, there is no reason to eat them: the mushrooms are certainly not taken recreationally.

The Aztecs were in such awe of the mushrooms that they called them *teonanacatl*, which translates as 'divine flesh'. Today they are used ritually not only by the Mazatecs, but also by the Nahua Indians of Puebla and the Tarascana of Michoacan, specifically in religious and divinatory rites. In all cases, the mushrooms are taken at night in rituals accompanied by chants and invocations. Interestingly, although psychoactive mushrooms also grow in South America, they do not appear to be used ritually.

Peyote and Mushrooms

ABOVE *When Native Americans attempted to re-establish traditional use of peyote in the late 19th century, the government objected.*

✧✧

CENTRE *Huichol yarn painting representing the visionary world that could be entered by the peyote-taker.*

✧✧

OPPOSITE ABOVE *Lewis Carroll used his knowledge of mind-altering mushrooms when he wrote* Alice in Wonderland.

✧✧

OPPOSITE BELOW *Aztec shaman invokes a spirit by eating a sacred mushroom.*

MORNING-GLORY

The morning-glory species *Rivea corymbosa* was known to the Aztecs as *ololiuhqui*, and they regarded the plant as a divinity. The seeds of this well-known flowering vine contain ergot alkaloids related to d-lysergic acid diethylamide, better known as LSD. However, the effects of morning-glory seeds are generally of shorter duration than an LSD experience, lasting only six hours.

RIGHT *Tlaloc fresco of a morning-glory plant. Streams of precious water flow from the flowers.*

❖❖

ABOVE *Morning-glory. In 1651 a Spanish physician wrote that Aztec priests ate morning-glory in order to receive messages from the gods.*

❖❖

Effects

Often associated with nausea, intake of the seeds can produce a sensation of bright lights and colour patterns, feelings of euphoria, and often profound states of peace and relaxation.

Usage

Today, morning-glory is used by Zapotec shamans to treat sickness or to acquire powers of divination. The seeds are carefully prepared for ritual use. They are ground on a stone to produce a type of flour which is added to cold water. The result is a beverage which is strained through cloth and then consumed. If the seeds are eaten whole they have no effect, passing through the body without producing hallucinations.

The Aztecs' use of morning-glory was suppressed after the Spanish conquest. Seeds were hidden to avoid persecution.

Ironically, as if to redeem the seeds' 'satanic' association in the minds of their Spanish conquerors, the Zapotecs of Oaxaca now refer to morning-glory seeds using Christian terminology, calling it 'Mary's herb' or 'the seed of the Virgin'.

Honan clan mask

Te clan figure

SAN PEDRO CACTUS

History

BELOW AND LEFT
A traditional mask and figure representing the Honan and Te clans, an old person, representing the clan's ancestors, and a man carrying his supply of hallucinogenic cactus.

❖

BELOW RIGHT
Peruvian textile showing figure in an axe headdress, surrounded by San Pedro cactus plants.

San Pedro cactus (*Trichocereus pachanoi*) is one of the most ancient magical plants of South America. Its use as a ritual sacrament dates back at least 3,000 years. In Peru, Spanish conquerors noticed shamans drinking a beverage made from the sap of the cactus.

Usage

It is used in a similar way today. The cactus is cut into slices, boiled for around seven hours in water, and then consumed. In Peru it is known simply as San Pedro; in Bolivia, *achuma*.

Effects

The cactus contains mescaline and initially produces drowsiness and a state of dreamy lethargy. However, this is followed by a remarkable lucidity of mental faculties. Finally, one may experience 'a telepathic sense of transmitting oneself across time and matter'.

Shamans in Peru and Bolivia utilize the cactus to contact spirits, to treat illness, to counteract the dangers of witchcraft, and for purposes of divination.

See page 72 for an account of the use of San Pedro cactus by the shaman Calderón.

Old person

Cactus carrier

BANISTERIOPSIS

The tree-climbing forest vine, *Banisteriopsis caapi*, is the pre-eminent sacred plant of South America. Its bark is brewed to make a beverage which is believed to allow direct contact with the supernatural realm, enabling shamans to contact ancestors or spirit helpers, and have initiatory visions.

Among the Jivaro of Ecuador, the drink made from banisteriopsis is called *natema*; elsewhere it is called *caapi*, *yaje* or *ayahuasca* – a term which translates as 'vine of the soul'.

Effects

The hallucinogenic qualities of banisteriopsis derive from the presence of the harmala alkaloids, harmaline and harmine. These were formerly known collectively as 'telepathine' because of their apparent capacity to stimulate extra-sensory perception.

In many subjects the drug produces the sensation of a 'flight of the soul', and intensely coloured and dramatic visions. Shamans utilizing *ayahuasca* report encounters with supernatural beings. (The Conibo say it helps them to see demons in the air. Among the Jivaro, shamans have reported having visions of giant anacondas and jaguars, rolling over and over through the rain forest.)

Usage

On a basic level, banisteriopsis is simply considered to be a powerful medicine, a means of healing, and a way of acquiring special knowledge.
It is used to recover the souls of sick patients, or to ask the spirits about the cause of bewitchment. In sorcery,  it may be used to allow a black magician to change into a bird or animal, in order to cause harm to someone.

Visions

The sacred drug also has the role of allowing shamans to participate in their own cosmology, to 'become one with the mythic world of the Creation'.

The Cashinahua regard the visions they experience as portents of things to come. They view the sacrament as 'a fearsome thing': something regarded with awe and very much respected. The Jivaro, meanwhile, consider that their spirit helpers, *tsentsak*, can only be seen in *natema*-induced visions and since disease is caused primarily by witchcraft, the sacred drug allows access to the sources of the trouble. Some *tsentsak* spirits also provide a type of psychic shield against magical attack.

ABOVE *Banisteriopsis is claimed to enhance telepathic abilities. One tribe described cars to a visiting anthropologist, without ever having physically seen any!*

❖

TOBACCO

Strictly speaking, tobacco is an intoxicant rather than a hallucinogen, although it is used shamanically in some parts of South America.

Campa Indians

The Campa Indians of the Peruvian rain forest combine tobacco and *ayahuasca* as a shamanic sacrament, but regard the tobacco in itself as a source of power. Used in nocturnal rituals, the combination produces an altered consciousness in which the shaman's voice takes on an eerie quality: the shaman's soul may go to some distant place, but the words themselves are those of the spirits, the trance allowing direct communication. 'When the shaman sings he is only repeating what he hears the spirits sing,' writes Gerald Weiss; 'he is merely singing along with them. At no time is he possessed by a spirit, since Campa culture does not include a belief in spirit possession.'[6]

The following shaman-song indicates that tobacco is revered in its own right:

❧❧

Tobacco, tobacco, pure tobacco,
It comes from River's Beginning
Kaokiti, the hawk, brings it to you
Its flowers are flying, tobacco
It comes to your [or our] aid, tobacco
Tobacco, tobacco, pure tobacco
Kaokiti, the hawk, is its owner.

❧❧

Warao Indians

The Warao Indian shamans of Venezuela, meanwhile, undertake periods of fasting and then smoke large cigars made of strong, local tobacco to induce a state of narcotic trance. The Warao believe that the Earth is surrounded by water, and that both the Earth and ocean in turn are covered by a celestial vault. At the cardinal and inter-cardinal points, the vault rests on a series of mountains. Supreme spirits (*kanobos*) dwell in these mountains at the edge of the world.

A Wishiratu's Journey

The shaman-priest, or *wishiratu*, is able to visit the *kanobos* during tobacco-induced trance journeys, even though the journeys are themselves fraught with such an assortment of obstacles and perils that one would hardly think them worthwhile!

To begin with, the shaman journeys towards the manaca palm (the shamanic tree of all *wishiratus*) and then travels to a series of waterholes where he can drink and purify himself. He then has to clear an abyss where jaguars, alligators, sharks and spear-bearing demons threaten to destroy him. He is also likely to encounter sexually provocative women, whom he must resist, and a giant hawk with a savage beak and flapping wings. These the shaman must pass by without temptation or fear, and only then is he nearing his goal:

Finally, the candidate shaman has to pass through a hole in an enormous tree trunk with rapidly opening and closing doors. He hears the voice of his guide and companion from the other side of the trunk, for this spirit has already cleared the dangerous passage and now encourages the fearful novice to follow his example. The candidate jumps through the clashing doors and looks around inside the hollow tree. There he beholds a huge serpent with four colourful horns and a fiery-red luminous ball on the tip of her protruding tongue. This serpent has a servant with reptilian body and human head, whom the candidate sees carrying away the bones of novices who have failed to clear the clashing doors.

The novice hurries outside and finds himself at the end of the cosmos. His patron kanobo's *mountain rises before him. Here he will be given a small house of his own, where he may sojourn in his future trances to consult with the* kanobo, *and where eventually he will come to live forever upon successful completion of his shaman's life on Earth.[7]*

ABOVE *Iroquois man smoking a pipe. The pipe was symbolic of peace and brotherhood.*

❧❧

Tobacco, Coca and Snuff

ABOVE TOP *Amazon Indians using tubes to inhale snuff.*

❖

ABOVE *Xingu river people in Brazil smoking
tobacco and taking ebena snuff.*

❖

CENTRE *An 1832 painting of North American Mandan
Indians during the sun ceremony. After smoking coca and
tobacco to induce visions, young males undergo voluntary
torture to prove manhood and seek out spirits.*

❖

ABOVE OPPOSITE *Makuna Indians' hangover cure:
hot pepper juice used as snuff!*

❖

BELOW OPPOSITE *Greeting and exchanging
coca in Colombia.*

EDUARDO CALDERÓN: *a Peruvian Healer*

Eduardo Calderón was a Peruvian shaman whose cosmology included Christian as well as native Indian elements.

Calderón was born in Trujillo in 1930 and grew up in a Spanish-speaking Roman Catholic family. Initially, he hoped to study religion or medicine; later he took a course in fine arts in Lima.

Apprenticeship

Both of Calderón's grandfathers were *curanderos* from the Peruvian highlands, and he too had yearnings in this direction. He began to have dreams urging him to 'prepare himself', and when he was 22, he was cured of an ailment by a folk-healer after orthodox medicine failed.

Another influence on Calderón's spiritual development was the uncle of his second wife, who was a *curandero*. At the age of 24, Calderón began an apprenticeship with the uncle, and was soon able to establish himself as a *curandero* in his own right.

San Pedro Cactus

San Pedro cactus is grown mainly in the region around Huancabamba, close to the border between Peru and Ecuador. Many shamans make pilgrimages to the area to obtain their sacraments.

Calderón believed that the San Pedro cactus, and magical herbs in general, had great shamanic value: 'The herbs have their spirits — because they speak [and] direct the activities in the realm of curanderismo during the nocturnal session … [the spirits] can advise or warn him.'[8]

However, he also believed that the healer could emit a power to the plants, infusing them with the intellectual and spiritual qualities of humankind. He claimed that the San Pedro and other magical plants provided a medium by which the healer's contact with the Earth was renewed in a reciprocal flow of energy.

Mesa

One of the most intriguing facets of Calderón's healing sessions was his *mesa*. This magical altar had two 'fields', representing zones of good and evil, and also a neutral zone where the opposing forces were held in balance.

The polarities of the *mesa* were crucial to Calderón's healing power, because associated with each zone were artefacts of different symbolic value. The smaller left-hand zone, associated with Satan, had three demonic staffs. The right-hand zone, ruled by Christ, had artefacts representative of positive magic: images of saints, holy water, various perfumes and cans of San Pedro infusion. Christ also had eight staffs allocated to him, including the sword of St Paul and the sword of St James the Elder.

In the neutral zone were objects of magical neutrality: a glass jar containing magical herbs, a crystal mirror, and a statue of St Cyprian, ruler of the neutral zone.

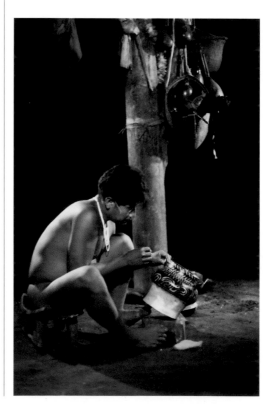

LEFT *Decorating a pot used for hallucinatory drugs.*

ABOVE *Calderón and his* mesa. *In front is a can of San Pedro juice.*

Healing

Healing sessions began at night. Calderón would undertake various ceremonial activities from 10am until midnight and the diagnosis, aided by the visionary effects of San Pedro, could last until 4am. Any night of the week was suitable for a healing ceremony except Monday, when it was believed that dead souls from purgatory were likely to be roaming about.

Following the ceremonial chants and invocations, which lasted until midnight, all present took San Pedro. For Calderón, as the *curandero*, this infusion 'activated' the artefacts of the *mesa*, enabling him to 'see' the cause of witchcraft or bad luck afflicting his client. Once the cause of evil had been perceived in this magical way, a ritual could then be carried out as a method of exorcism.

Calderón explained that San Pedro enabled him to 'visualize' and open up a 'sixth sense', thus allowing him to have an intimate perception of his client's psyche:

The subconscious is a superior part [of Man] ... a kind of bag where the individual has stored all his memories ... all his valuations. One must try ... to make the individual 'jump out' of his conscious mind. That is the principal task of curanderismo. By means of the magical plants and the chants and the search for the roots of the problem, the subconscious of the individual is opened like a flower.[9]

Anthropologist Douglas Sharon summed up the healing process succinctly. 'The hallucinogenic San Pedro cactus is experienced as the catalyst that enables the *curandero* to transcend the limitations placed on ordinary mortals; to activate all his senses; project his spirit or soul; ascend and descend into the supernatural realms; identify and do battle with the sources of illness ... "to see".'[10]

6

THE
SHAMANS SPEAK

T here have been many shamans throughout history, each with a special way of perceiving the world. Many of them we can know only through myth, legend or song, but some, such as Eduardo Calderón, have left their mark on cultural history as individuals, and their stories have been recorded for others to appreciate.

In this chapter are further profiles of notable shamans who have made a unique contribution to the visionary perspective. Each, in his or her own way, has experienced a special encounter which led to a feeling of renewal, a revitalizing of both the inner and outer worlds.

BLACK ELK

Black Elk was an Oglala Sioux holy man — a *wichasha wakon* — who was part of the Messianic movement that ended with the massacre at Wounded Knee in 1890. Born in 1863, he was the second cousin of Crazy Horse, the famous chieftain who led the Sioux in the Indian wars.

Biography

Black Elk recounted the remarkable visionary episodes which had transformed his life to a white man, John G. Neihardt. Neihardt was welcomed by the Oglala Sioux as an intermediary to communicate Black Elk's visions to a broader audience. Black Elk's son, Ben, acted as a translator.

Neihardt published *Black Elk Speaks* in 1932. It has been translated into several languages. Black Elk died in 1950.

First Vision

For Black Elk, the call to shamanism came early in life. When he was five, he had a spontaneous shamanic experience. As he looked up at the sky, two human figures seemed to descend from the clouds, singing a sacred song. Black Elk recalled:

❦

I sat there gazing at them, and they were coming from the place where the giant lives [north]. But when they were very close to me, they wheeled about toward where the Sun goes down, and suddenly they were geese. Then they were gone, and the rain came with a big wind and a roaring. I did not tell this vision to anyone. I liked to think about it, but I was afraid to tell it.[1]

❦

OPPOSITE *Shamans' experiences provide us with a fascinating insight into alternative views of the world.*

❖

RIGHT *Black Elk (left) with his father.*

❖

The Call

When he was nine, further revelations occurred. Black Elk was resting in his tepee when he heard a voice say distinctly: 'It is time, now they are calling you.' He went outside and looked around, but there was no one there. He noticed, however, that his legs were hurting him.

The following morning, Black Elk went riding with some other boys. He stopped by a creek and when he got off his horse, his legs crumpled beneath him. His friends helped him back on to his horse, but he became quite sick and seemed badly swollen all over.

The next day, as he lay in his tepee looking out through the opening, two figures appeared to come down through the clouds. They were the same figures he had seen four years earlier.

Each now carried a long spear, and from the points of these a jagged lightning flashed. They came down to the ground this time and stood a little way off and looked at me and said: 'Hurry! Come! Your grandfathers are calling you!' [2]

ABOVE *Black Elk's son Ben, photographed as a performer in 1955.*

Shamanic Journey

Black Elk 'rose' to his feet, finding his legs did not hurt and he felt 'very light'. He was clearly experiencing a sense of dissociation. He now began a classical shamanic journey:

I went outside the tepee, and yonder where the men with flaming spears were going, a little cloud was coming very fast. It came and stopped and took me and turned back to where it came from, flying fast. And when I looked down I could see my mother and my father yonder, and I felt sorry to be leaving them.
Now suddenly there was nothing but a world of cloud, and we three were there alone in the middle of a great white plain with snowy hills and mountains staring at us; and it was very still; but there were whispers. [3]

HORSES

Black Elk now had a dramatic and very beautiful vision of a dozen majestic horses, with lightning flashing in their manes and thunder roaring from their nostrils.

In three further visions, different coloured groups of horses danced across the sky, the heavens reverberating with the stamping of their hooves. The horses then transformed 'into animals of every kind', and disappeared to the four quarters of the world.

POWERS OF THE WORLD

Rising before him in the clouds, Black Elk saw a tepee, with a rainbow as its open door. Inside, he could see six old men sitting in a row:

The two men with the spears now stood beside me, and the horses took their place in their quarters. And the oldest of the grandfathers spoke with a kind voice and said: 'Come right in and do not fear.' As he spoke, all the horses neighed to cheer me. So I went in and stood before the six, and they looked older than men could ever be: old like hills, like stars.
The oldest spoke again: 'Your grandfathers all over the world are having a council, and they have called you here to teach you.' [4]

Overcome by awe, Black Elk realized that the grandfathers were no ordinary ancestors: they were the powers of the world. They gave him a water-filled wooden cup (representing the powers of life), a bow (with the power to destroy), a herb (for healing), a peace-pipe with a seemingly live eagle on its stem, and a bright red stick which sprouted like a Tree of Life.

Black Elk then witnessed dramatic scenes of violence and renewal, representing the tragic future of the American Indians on the planet.

CENTRE OF THE WORLD

Black Elk was now transported to the centre of the world:

I was standing on the highest mountain of them all, and round about beneath me was the whole hoop of the world. And while I stood there, I saw more than I can tell and I understood more than I saw; for I was seeing in a sacred manner the shapes of all things in the spirit, and the shape of all shapes as they must live together like one being. And I saw that the sacred hoop of my people was one of many hoops that made one circle, wide as daylight and as starlight, and in the centre grew one mighty flowering tree to shelter all the children of one mother and one father. And I saw that it was holy.[5]

RETURN TO REALITY

As Black Elk returned to the tepee of the six grandfathers, there was much rejoicing. Black Elk was told that he must now return to his people, and suddenly:

I was in my own tepee, and inside I saw my mother and my father, bending over a sick boy that was myself. Then I was sitting up; and I was sad because my mother and my father didn't seem to know I had been so far away.[6]

Grounding the Visions

Black Elk initially kept his vision a secret, but found it a strain. A medicine man named Black Road was summoned to treat Black Elk's continuing malaise. When Black Elk told him what had happened, the medicine man directed him to perform his vision for everyone to see. The mythic encounter would have to be grounded in a 'horse dance'.

A short time after Black Elk's seventeenth birthday, preparations began.

ABOVE *Black Elk as an old man.*

The Horse Dance

With members of the tribe representing
characters in the vision, the major events of
Black Elk's experience were performed
ceremonially.

At one point, a remarkable thing happened.
All the horses in the village neighed in unison
and, as Black Elk looked up towards the
heavens, once again he beheld his vision. It
was as if the mythic world and the physical
world had become one:

Suddenly, as I sat there looking at the cloud, I saw
my vision yonder once again. I knew the real was
yonder and the darkened dream of it was here.[7]

Communal Happiness

Here was dramatic confirmation of Black Elk's
ceremonial undertaking to share his visions
with his people. Clearly the grandfathers had
observed the ritual re-enactment and were
well pleased. The peace-pipe was passed
around and a sense of renewal seemed to
pervade the community:

❖❖

I felt very happy, for I could see that my people were
all happier. Many crowded around me and said that
they or their relatives who had been feeling sick were
well again, and gave me many gifts. Even the horses
seemed to be healthier and happier
after the dance.[8]

❖❖

LUISAH TEISH

Luisah Teish was born in New Orleans of mixed African, Haitian, Choctaw and French ancestry. She is a dancer, choreographer, singer, shaman, healer and writer.

Teish (pronounced 'Teesh') describes herself as originally 'Louisiana Catholic': a polite expression for one who follows voodoo behind a thin veneer of Christianity.

Teish says that her entire childhood was filled with visions and intuitions, and the whispered guidance of a spirit guide.

ABOVE *Raised in New Orleans, nominally a Roman Catholic, Teish increasingly became a practitioner of voodoo.*

❖❖

OPPOSITE *A shrine to the goddess Oshun in Nigeria. Teish feels a special bond with Oshun, who is the Nigerian counterpart of the Roman goddess Venus.*

Eguns and Orishas

For Luisah Teish, the spiritual universe offers contact with the consciousness of the ancestors (*eguns*) and the consciousness of Nature (*orishas*). *Orishas* are elemental energies such as wind, fire, river and ocean.

Teish says *orishas* are like 'friends with extra-human powers who can help you.'

Dance

Teish says that learning traditional native dance helped her to free her psychic energies, and tap into her ancestral heritage.

For Teish, magical ceremonial dance has a very powerful effect. As she explains:

❖—❖

Suddenly I find I'm dancing off-rhythm, and an ancestor or a spirit is there. You are not really in control of your body. You find you are now on the wall; on the ceiling; over there somewhere; watching your body performing. It's very invigorating. The body seems to be able to do things in trance that you cannot do when you're fully conscious.[9]

❖—❖

Magic

People come to Teish for spiritual advice, or for wealth and love charms. She claims to be able to reverse black magic, but rarely inflicts harmful magic on others.

Universal Awareness

Teish believes her main role is now to help others tune into a universal religious awareness that goes beyond sectarian differences. She focuses on helping to build an environmental understanding that acknowledges the sanctity of Nature. 'I do have a basic faith in Nature's tendency to survive. The closer we get to the possibility of total destruction, the more Nature will cause a change in basic consciousness to come about.'[10]

Other Shamans

OPPOSITE LEFT *Mongol Chahar shaman beats his drum.*

❖❖

OPPOSITE RIGHT *Sakuddei tribe shaman from Siberut Island in Indonesia. Shamans are the political leaders of their tribes. Shamanism in Indonesia functions against a background of Islam.*

❖❖

OPPOSITE BELOW *A Brazilian Yanomamo shaman communing with the spirits. Shamanism is part of daily life in South America.*

❖❖

RIGHT *Taoist shaman in a trance, Taiwan. Taoism took over the old shamanic religion and incorporated many of its elements.*

❖❖

BELOW LEFT *Solon shaman wearing a copper mask.*

❖❖

BELOW RIGHT *In most tribes, shamans are usually either all males or all females. In Korea, shamans are female.*

BROOKE MEDICINE EAGLE

Brooke Medicine Eagle provides an interesting example of how shamanism can link the old and the new. She is of Sioux and Nez Perce descent, but is also university educated, and interested in holistic health therapies. She sees herself as a bridge between different cultures.

The Feldenkrais Method

Moshe Feldenkrais developed a system of body movements aimed at undoing people's emotional and cultural programming. Those using the Feldenkrais method often speak of feeling exhilarated and more alive in their movements.

For Brooke Medicine Eagle, this concept is also part of shamanism. She emphasizes the importance of expanding beyond artificial boundaries and limitations of movement. For her, the Western way of thinking often tends to be restrictive and inhibiting:

❥❦

Most of us think of life as a path, the best being the straight and narrow, where we can plod along without change. I think life is more like flying a glider ... The challenge is to play on the edge — the edge of the unformed. Part of the shaman's way is that exquisite balance: between light and dark, in and out, left and right, formless and formed.[11]

❥❦

Neuro-Linguistic Programming

A neuro-linguistic programming (NLP) therapist observes the client's behavioural and linguistic patterns, and endeavours to guide the person beyond personal limitations to new levels of awareness and personal effectiveness.

For Brooke Medicine Eagle, NLP has highlighted the way that Western culture leads so often to a programming of behaviour and a perpetuation of habits. The trouble with this is that the more we reside in our habitual behaviour patterns, the less able we are to be open to acquiring new knowledge. This, too, is where shamanism can be beneficial. 'My work', she says, 'is about finding ways to help us move as shamans have: to challenge the darkness; to awaken ourselves by breaking through daily habitual form into spirit.'

OPPOSITE LEFT
Brooke Medicine Eagle was brought up on the Crow Reservation in Montana.

❖

BELOW *Chief Joseph of the Nez Perce, great-great-uncle of Brooke Medicine Eagle.*

Vision Quest

Brooke Medicine Eagle took her shamanic vision quest with an 85-year-old Cheyenne shaman called The Woman Who Knows, near the Black Hills of South Dakota. This region has been used for hundreds of years by the Sioux and Cheyenne as a location for the vision quest.

Here Brooke Medicine Eagle underwent the traditional preparation of fasting and cleansing, before being left alone. As she rested, she suddenly became aware of the presence of a woman with long, black, braided hair, dressed in buckskin. The woman said that the land was in trouble and needed a new sense of balance, more feminine, nurturing energy and less male aggression.

It became abundantly clear that this being was a spirit teacher:

❖

Her feet stayed where they were, but she shot out across the sky in a rainbow arc that covered the heavens, her head at the top of the arc. And then the lights that formed that rainbow began to die out, almost like fireworks in the sky, died out from her feet and died out and died out. And she was gone.[12]

❖

Mission

For Brooke Medicine Eagle, the visitation indicated how she could be of service.

❖

[The spirit teacher] felt that I would be a carrier of the message between the two cultures [white and Indian]. And in a sense, all of us in this generation can be that. We can help bridge that gap, build that bridge into the new age of balance.[13]

❖

This, then, is Brooke Medicine Eagle's particular path in shamanism: the knowledge that the Earth will benefit from more feminine energy, more caring. 'We need to allow, to be receptive, to surrender, to serve,' she says. 'The whole society, men and women, needs that balance to bring ourselves into balance.'

SUN BEAR

A medicine man of Chippewa descent, Sun Bear was by no means a typical shaman. He worked in Hollywood, had a thriving practice in workshops and vision quests, and wrote several books. He felt that his path was to reach out to other cultures and to share with them his vision for harmony on Earth.

Sun Bear, or Gheezis Mokwa, was born in 1929 on the White Earth Reservation in northern Minnesota. He learned native medicine from his uncles and brothers, but didn't actually practise it until he was 25 years old.

The Bear Tribe

After working for the Intertribal Council of Nevada as an economic development specialist, Sun Bear assisted in a native studies programme sponsored by the University of California at Davis, north of San Francisco. It was here, in 1970, that he founded the Bear Tribe. Most of the members were his former students from the Davis campus. Sun Bear maintained that he selected the name because 'the bear is one of the few animals that heals its own wounds' and he had in mind an organization whose members 'could all join together to help with the healing of the Earth.'[14]

The Bear Tribe is now located near Spokane in Washington. The community is largely self-sufficient.

Philosophy

Sun Bear summed up his philosophy in his book *The Medicine Wheel*. He said: 'We all share the same Earth Mother, regardless of race or country of origin, so let us learn the ways of love, peace and harmony and see the good paths in life.'[15]

Sun Bear believed it was no longer appropriate to restrict the Native American teachings to his own people. His global view espoused restoring a sense of balance, and increased ecological awareness:

If you teach people to find a better balance within themselves, how to be stronger, centre their life, and go forward with a good balance upon the Earth Mother, then that is a healing. You take away all the little pains when you teach people to become self-reliant ... When people have centred themselves, they know that they can draw power from the universe.[16]

ABOVE *Sun Bear founded the Bear Tribe, a community running an extensive workshop programme.*

Role

Sun Bear believed that, as a medicine man, he was a protector of the Earth Mother, and an embodiment of the spirits of the Earth. The resurgence of interest in shamanism is a reflection of the fact that humankind has increasingly fallen out of harmony with Nature. This is where Sun Bear felt he had a special role to play. His aim, when working with participants on vision quests, was 'to teach them how to make prayers and ceremonies for communication with the natural forces, so that they can start learning to restore their own powers.'[18]

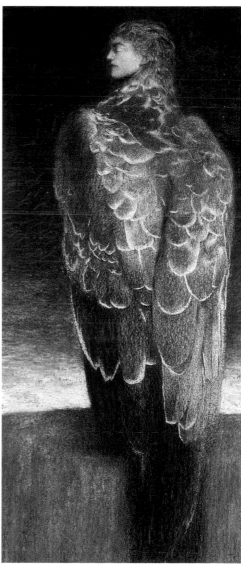

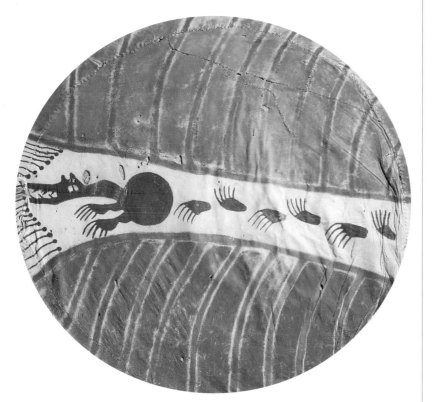

ABOVE *Shield cover painted with a bear. The symbols were designed to protect the shield's owner.*

✣

RIGHT *Spirits may be attracted by the wearing of an animal or bird mask.*

Vision Quest

Sun Bear drew strongly on authentic Native American traditions, such as the vision quest.

This entails going to a location where the energy seems vibrant, and where spirits might appear. It is the presence of spirits, in dreams or in visions, that provides an authentic sense of personal direction. But largely this is up to oneself. As Sun Bear said, 'Each medicine man has to follow his own medicine and the dreams and visions that give him power.'

Another way of attracting the spirits is to don an animal mask, for example that of a buffalo, bear or eagle. By doing this, one feels a strong surge of spiritual energy, a profound sense of transformation: 'You literally become that entity, that power … The spirit comes into you completely, to the extent that you are no longer there, and you are able to communicate what the spirit is feeling. That is what the ceremonies are about at the deepest depth.'[17]

What is Not True Shamanism?

Some native practices may be confused
with shamanism. Strictly speaking,
shamanism is active: shamans seek out
spiritual encounters on a visionary journey.
In mediumistic practices, subjects may also
go into a trance, but then act as a channel
for the spirits. These pictures show
non-shamanic practices.

RIGHT *A Dinka witchdoctor dances
in a trance, Sudan.*

❖❖

OPPOSITE *Voodoo. A fire dancer
in Haiti.*

❖❖

BELOW *A Tibetan oracle prophesies
future events and actions. She is
believed to be infallible.*

❖❖

BELOW RIGHT *Witchcraft. In this
Greek myth, Circe prepares a magic potion
to turn Odysseus into a pig.*

Shamans and Mediums

We should try to differentiate shamanism from mediumism, since both involve trance states. Essentially, shamanism is active and mediumism passive. Shamanism involves a *going forth* of the spirit, whereas mediumism involves a *coming in* of the divine force.

Mediumism includes characters such as the Pythian oracle of ancient Delphi, who made divinely inspired pronouncements in trance at the Temple of Apollo, through to modern forms of spiritualism, such as 'channelling', where ancient sages are believed to communicate with the living through the body of the possessed

trance medium. Also within the mediumistic category is the darker aspect of voodoo in Haiti, where 'divine horsemen', or *loa* divinities, are said to descend upon the trance subjects during their ecstatic dance rituals and 'ride' them in a frenzy.

In mediumistic trance, subjects do not recall their visionary episodes, having acted as passive channels for the received revelations. In shamanism, on the other hand, the ecstatic has full consciousness of the altered state, and takes complete responsibility for what transpires during the visionary journey.

7

CAN WE BE
SHAMANS IN THE WEST?

ABOVE
*A modern Western
interpretation of a
shaman with the familiar
horned headdress and
crutch representing the
wounded healer.*

*W̲hat lessons can we learn from the shamanic
practices, and to what extent can we apply the
shamanic perspective in a modern urban setting? Is it
possible to adapt authentic shamanic concepts to our
postmodern cultural frameworks without trivializing or
denigrating their essential message?*

RIGHT
*The Dream by Odilon
Redon 1840–1916, who
was inspired to paint
visionary representations
of the inner quest for
the spirit.*

Turning Back the Clock

Personally, I don't think it is either possible, or appropriate, to try to turn back the cultural clock. Shamanism is traditionally the religious expression of a nomadic era of hunter-gatherers and most of us, in the West, live in industrialized cities or towns, surrounded by numerous manifestations of complex technology. Furthermore, unlike the wandering shaman, prone to the vagaries of the weather and seasonal variations in food supply, we have a comparatively settled existence and, for the most part, buy our food in a supermarket or store!

Shamanism originates in comparatively isolated, pre-literate societies, and it is a fantasy to endeavour to transpose the world of the shaman to our own contemporary setting in any literal way.

But having said that, I do believe that shamanism has a basic world-view and approach to our planetary existence which can be applied in a modern context.

Searching

It seems to me that the resurgence of interest in native mythologies, altered states of consciousness, and the mysticism of the East, all reflect a widespread yearning for a religious framework based on deep inner experience. Shamanism can certainly help us here.

The symbolism of the World Tree, used in visualization, is of universal appeal, and does not imply an imposed belief system. The root-tunnel which leads towards the light is a motif of transition: one uses it to journey into a realm of consciousness which might otherwise be inaccessible. Whether we call this level of awareness our 'subconscious mind' or our 'inner self', or use some other comparable term to describe it, it is clear that the shamanic technique opens up the possibility for each of us to discover our own inner mythology, to explore our own transpersonal archetypes, to find our own dreamtime.

Here are our own inner gods – the voices of our soul – and by discovering them and by communicating with them, we have access to a deep and often profound spiritual reality that bears its own sense of authenticity. We no longer require a formal religious framework or belief system based on some form of empty, inherited doctrine. Our religion, once again, has become based on what we can feel, what we can know.

Energy

One aspect of shamanism (and a perception I believe we can all be enriched by, irrespective of our personal religious dispositions) is a feeling for the sheer 'aliveness' of the universe. Gone is any distinction between animate or inanimate. The whole universe is ablaze with energy.

All forms are perceived as interconnected, with a universal life-force underlying all. This is a truly holistic vision because energy is matter, and matter is spirit. Our purpose in applying a shamanic orientation within our own lives then becomes one of finding for ourselves our individual role for assisting the 'universal flow'.

Exploration

Increasingly, the holistic health movement is urging us to discover our own inner truths, heed our own inner voice, and take responsibility for our actions.

Certainly, like shamans, there are times when we will explore uncharted waters, encounter obstacles, and perhaps wander down blind alleys. But hopefully, at all times, we will also venture into sacred realms which extend well beyond familiar realms of consciousness. Some of us have experienced this already through meditation, prayer, or by exploring psychedelics. The experience has often been profound and life-transforming.

Allied to this, and also reinforced by the shaman's approach, is the need we all have to find the god, and goddess, within ourselves. We must seek a healing balance of male and female energies within our being and, perhaps most importantly, recognize the sanctity of Nature.

Against Nature?

Nature

Shamanism is, if nothing else, a religious perspective which venerates Nature. In this age of industrial pollution and damage to the ozone layer, shamanism urges us to attune our religious beliefs to working with Nature and not against it.

An Attitude

I believe, then, that one can act as a type of modern shaman by addressing these principles in our personal life. It is not so much a matter of theatre or ceremonial, but a shift in basic attitudes. Shamanism can teach us much, simply by leading us back to a core simplicity in our lives. We all share a common destiny on this planet, we are all born of Mother Earth and ultimately we are accountable, both to each other and to future generations, if the precious balance between humankind and Nature is jeopardized.

To this extent, then, we can all be like shamans while also being true to ourselves. As Sun Bear said: 'We all share the same Earth Mother, regardless of race or country of origin, so let us learn the ways of love, peace and harmony, and seek the good paths in life.'

It is a message that each of us can truly take to heart.

ABOVE *Over-exploitation of the land has caused the desertification of large parts of Africa.*

❖❖

CENTRE *Inside the destroyed nuclear reactor at Chernobyl. Are the risks associated with nuclear power acceptable?*

❖❖

BELOW *Amazon rain forest chopped down to accommodate a tin mine. The destruction of the rain forests is a serious ecological problem.*

NOTES AND REFERENCES

Chapter 1

1 Abbé Henri Breuil, 'The Palaeolithic Age', in René Huyghe (ed.) *Larousse Encyclopedia of Prehistoric and Ancient Art*, 1962, p. 30
2 Joan Halifax, *Shaman: The Wounded Healer*, 1982, p. 6
3 Ralph Linton, *Culture and Mental Disorders*, 1956, p. 124
4 Joan Halifax, op. cit., p. 14
5 Waldemar Bogoras, *The Chukchee*, 1909, p. 421
6 See H. S. Sullivan, *Conceptions of Modern Psychiatry*, Norton, New York, 1953, pp. 151–2
7 Mircea Eliade, *Shamanism*, 1972, p. 13
8 Mircea Eliade, *Birth and Rebirth*, 1964, p. 102
9 W. A. Lessa and E. Z. Vogt (eds.), *Reader in Comparative Religion*, 1972, p. 388
10 Ibid., p. 389

Chapter 2

1 Mircea Eliade, *Shamanism*, 1972, p. 198
2 G. M. Vasilevich, 'Early Concepts about the Universe Among the Evenks', 1963, p. 58
3 Joan Halifax, *Shamanic Voices*, 1979, p. 183
4 See W. A. Lessa and E. Z. Vogt (eds.) *Reader in Comparative Religion*, 1972, Ch. 9.
5 See A. P. Elkin's classic work, *Aboriginal Men of High Degree*, 1977, p. 63
6 Sue Ingram, *Structures of Shamanism in Indonesia and Malaysia*, 1972, p. 127
7 Kenneth Cohen, 'Taoist Shamanism', *The Laughing Man, Vol. 2, No. 4*, p. 49
8 Larry G. Peters, 'The Tamang Shamanism of Nepal', 1987, p. 171
9 For an account of Deguchi Onisaburo's trance experiences see Carmen Blacker, *The Catalpa Bow*, 1975.

Chapter 3

1 Mircea Eliade, *Shamanism*, 1972, p. 261
2 Ibid., p. 272
3 Ibid., p. 273
4 G. M. Vasilevich, 'Early Concepts about the Universe Among the Evenks', 1963
5 Asen Balikci, 'Shamanistic Behaviour Amongst the Netsilik Eskimos', 1967, p. 200
6 Joan Halifax, *Shamanic Voices*, 1979, p. 121
7 Ibid., p. 122

Chapter 4

1 Michael Harner, *The Way of the Shaman*, 1980, p. 62
2 Mircea Eliade, *Shamanism*, 1972, p. 132
3 Carmen Blacker, *The Catalpa Bow*, 1975, p. 25
4 Joan Halifax, *Shamanic Voices*, 1979, p. 176
5 Ibid., p. 177
6 Michael Harner, op. cit., p. 51
7 Mircea Eliade, op. cit., p. 172
8 Ibid., p. 52
9 Joan Halifax, op. cit., p. 30
10 Nevill Drury, *Music and Musicians*, 1980, p. 51
11 Joan Halifax, op. cit., p. 30
12 Ibid., p. 185
13 Michael Harner, op. cit., p. 3

Chapter 5

1 Peter T. Furst, *Hallucinogens and Culture*, p. 112
2 Quoted in R. E. Schultes and A. Hofmann, *Plants of the Gods*, 1979, p. 134
3 R. G. Wasson, *The Wondrous Mushroom*, 1980, p. xvi
4 Henry Munn, 'The Mushrooms of Language' in Michael Harner (ed.) *Hallucinogens and Shamanism*, 1973, p. 88
5 Ibid., p. 90

6 Michael Harner, *The Way of the Shaman*, 1980, p. 44
7 Peter T. Furst (ed.) *Flesh of the Gods*, 1972, p. 64
8 Douglas Sharon, 'The San Pedro Cactus in Peruvian Folk Healing', 1972, p. 122
9 Ibid., p. 131
10 Ibid., p. 130

Chapter 6

1 John G. Neihardt, *Black Elk Speaks*, 1972, p. 16
2 Quoted in Stephen Larsen, *The Shaman's Doorway*, 1976, p. 104
3 Ibid., p. 105
4 Ibid.
5 Ibid., p. 36
6 Ibid., p. 39
7 Stephen Larsen, op. cit., p. 115
8 Ibid., p. 116
9 Personal Communication, November 1984
10 Mimi Albert, 'Out of Africa', January/February 1987
11 Michele Jamal, *Shape Shifters*, 1987, pp. 164, 165
12 Joan Halifax, *Shamanic Voices*, 1979, pp. 89–90
13 Michele Jamal, op. cit., pp. 89–90
14 Robert Neubert, 'Sun Bear – Walking in Balance on the Earth Mother', p. 10
15 Sun Bear and Wabun, *The Medicine Wheel*, 1980, p. xiii
16 Ron Boyer, 'The Vision Quest', p. 63
17 Ibid., p. 60
18 Ibid., p. 62

ACKNOWLEDGEMENTS

Archiv für Kunst und Geschichte, London: ROYAL ONTARIO MUSEUM, TORONTO 2, 48. **Bridgeman Art Library:** F. LABISSE COLLECTION, NEUILLY 85b; LAUROS-GIRAUDON 89. **The British Library:** 37t. **Cameron Collection:** 43, 46tm, 47tl, 47bl. **Amon Carter Museum:** 18. **Edward Curtis:** 25tr, 74, 83. **Nevill Drury:** 58b, 79t. **e.t.archive:** 50b; BIBLIOTHEQUE NATIONALE 61. **Mary Evans Picture Library:** 52b. **Werner Forman Archive:** 21bl, 36, 50t, 67br; ANCHORAGE MUSEUM AND ART GALLERY: 7br; BUFFALO BILL HISTORICAL CENTER, WYOMING: 51r; EUGENE CHESTOW TRUST: 7tr; DENVER ART MUSEUM, COLORADO: 42b; FIELD MUSEUM OF NATURAL HISTORY, CHICAGO: 85t; NATIONAL MUSEUM, DENMARK 41t; PROVINCIAL MUSEUM, VICTORIA, CANADA: 25bl. **Fortean Picture Library:** DR ELMAR GRUBER 6/7, 64/5. **The Hutchison Library:** 80tr; CHRISTINA DODWELL: 11t, 18, 23; H.R.DORIG: 59; SARAH ERRINGTON: 40l, 86tr, 87; JOHN GOLDBLATT: 78r; NICK HASLAM: 86bl; CRISPIN HUGHES: 91t; VICTORIA IVLEVA: 22, 91m; R. IAN LLOYD: 81tr; MICHAEL MCINTYRE: 7mr, 27, 32tr, 33tr, 34–56, 58t, 60, 81br; BRIAN MOSER: 14, 20mr, 21t, 28, 29, 33bl, 71br; 72b; MOSER/TAYLER: 71tr; SARAH MURRAY: 15; CARLOS PASINI: 70m, 80b; ANDRE SINGER: 49t, 55r; IVAN STRASBURG: 10b, 13tl, 20tl; LIBA TAYLOR: 26, 34/5t; CHRISTOPHER TORDAI: 12; ISABELLA TREE: 21mr, 32tl, 54; JESCO VON PUTTKAMER: 91b. **Images Colour Library:** 8, 56/7, 88; COVELL PUBLISHING/HORIZON: 17, 24; DOUGLASS BAGLIN/HORIZON: 30/1. **Wernher Krutein:** 82tl. **Alan Lee:** 38r. **Tom McBride:** 84. **National Museum of Canada:** 56l. **Range Picture Library/Bettman Archive:** 55l. **Douglas Sharon:** 73tl. **The Smithsonian Institute:** 75, 77tr.

Every effort has been made to find the copyright owners of the material used. However if any omissions have been made, we would be glad to hear from the copyright owners so that acknowledgement can be made in any future edition.

BIBLIOGRAPHY

Albert, M., 'Out of Africa', *Yoga Journal*, January/February, 1987.

Andrews, L., *Medicine Woman*, Harper & Row, San Francisco, 1981.
- *Flight of the Seventh Moon*, Harper & Row, San Francisco, 1984.
- *Jaguar Woman*, Harper & Row, San Francisco, 1985.
- *Star Woman*, Warner Books, New York, 1986.
- *Crystal Woman*, Warner Books, New York, 1987.

Balikci, A., 'Shamanistic Behaviour Among the Netsilik Eskimos', in J. Middleton (ed.) *Magic, Witchcraft and Curing*, Natural History Press, New York, 1967.

Bharati, A. (ed.), *The Realm of the Extra-Human*, Mounton, The Hague, 1976.

Blacker, C., *The Catalpa Bow*, Allen & Unwin, London, 1975.

Bogoras, W., *The Chukchee, Memoirs of the American Museum of Natural History*, Vol. XL, New York and Leiden, 1909.

Boyer, R., 'The Vision Quest', *The Laughing Man*, Vol. 2, No. 4.

Breuil, H., 'The Paleolithic Age' in *Larousse Encyclopedia of Prehistoric and Ancient Art*, Hamlyn, London, 1962.

Budapest, Z., *The Holy Book of Women's Mysteries, Parts One and Two*, Susan B. Anthony Coven #1 Coven, Los Angeles, 1979–80.

Castaneda, C., *The Teachings of Don Juan*, University of California Press, Berkeley, 1968.
- *A Separate Reality*, Simon & Schuster, New York, 1971.
- *Journey to Ixtlan*, Simon & Schuster, New York, 1972.
- *Tales of Power*, Simon & Schuster, New York, 1974.
- *A Second Ring of Power*, Simon & Schuster, New York, 1976.
- *The Eagle's Gift*, Simon & Schuster, New York, 1981.
- *The Fire from Within*, Simon & Schuster, New York, 1984.

Cohen, K., 'Taoist Shamanism', *The Laughing Man*, Vol. 2, No. 4, n.d.

Daab, R., 'An Interview with Lynn Andrews', *Magical Blend, No. 16*, 1987.

Das, P., 'Initiation by a Huichol Shaman', *The Laughing Man*, Vol. 2, No. 4, n.d.

De Mille, R., *Castaneda's Journey*, Capra Press, Santa Barbara, 1976.
- *The Don Juan Papers*, Ross-Erikson, Santa Barbara, 1980.

Doore, G. (ed.), *Shaman's Path*, Shambhala, Boston, 1988.

Drury, N., *Don Juan, Mescalito and Modern Magic*, Routledge & Kegan Paul, London, 1978.
- *Inner Visions*, Routledge & Kegan Paul, London, 1979.
- *Music and Musicians*, Nelson, Melbourne, 1980.
- *The Shaman and the Magician*, Routledge & Kegan Paul, London, 1982.
- *Vision Quest*, Prism, Dorchester, 1984.
- *The Gods of Rebirth*, Prism, Bridport, 1988.
- 'The Shaman: Healer and Visionary', *Nature & Health*, Vol. 9, No. 2, Winter, 1988.
- *The Occult Experience*, Hale, London, 1987, and Avery, New York, 1989.

Durkheim, E., *The Elementary Forms of the Religious Life*, Allen & Unwin, London, 1915.

Eliade, M., *Birth and Rebirth*, Harper, New York, 1964.
- *Shamanism*, Princeton University Press, New Jersey, 1972.

Elkin, A., *Aboriginal Men of High Degree*, University of Queensland Press, St Lucia, Brisbane, 1977.

Estrada, A., *Maria Sabina: Her Life and Chants*, Ross-Erikson, Santa Barbara, 1981.

Furst, P. T. (ed.), *Flesh of the Gods*, Allen & Unwin, London, 1972.
- *Hallucinogens and Culture*, Chandler & Sharp, San Francisco, 1976.

Grof, S., *Realms of the Human Unconscious*, Dutton, New York, 1976.

Halifax, J., *Shamanic Voices*, Dutton, New York, 1979.
- *Shaman: The Wounded Healer*, Crossroad, New York, 1982.

Harner, M., *The Jivaro*, Hale, London, 1972.
- *Hallucinogens and Shamanism*, Oxford University Press, New York, 1973.
- *The Way of the Shaman*, Harper & Row, San Francisco, 1980.

Hori, I., *Folk Religion in Japan*, University of Chicago Press, Chicago and London, 1968.

Ingram, S., *Structures of Shamanism in Indonesia and Malaysia*, (University of Sydney anthropology thesis), 1972.

Jamal, M., *Shape Shifters*, Arkana, New York and London, 1987.

Kalweit, H., *Dreamtime and Inner Space*, Shambhala, Boston, 1988.

La Barre, W., *The Ghost Dance*, Allen & Unwin, London, 1972

Larsen, S., *The Shaman's Doorway*, Harper & Row, New York, 1976.

Lessa, W. A. and Vogt, E. Z., *Reader in Comparative Religion*, Harper & Row, New York, 1972.

Lewis, I., *Ecstatic Religion*, Penguin, Harmondsworth, 1971.

Linton, R., *Culture and Mental Disorders*, Charles C. Thomas, Springfield, Illinois, 1956.

Michael, H. N. (ed.), *Studies in Siberian Shamanism*, University of Toronto Press, Toronto, 1963.

Middleton, J. (ed.), *Magic Witchcraft and Curing*, The Natural History Press, New York, 1967.

Munn, H., 'The Mushrooms of Language', in M. Harner (ed.), *Hallucinogens and Shamanism*, Oxford University Press, New York, 1973.

Neihardt, J. G., *Black Elk Speaks*, Pocket Books, New York, 1972.

Neubert, R., 'Sun Bear – Walking In Balance on the Earth Mother', *New Realities*, May/June 1987.

Noel, D. (ed.), *Seeing Castaneda*, Putnam, New York, 1976.

Noffke, W., 'Living in a Sacred Way: An Interview with Chequeesh, a Chumash Medicine Woman', *Shaman's Drum*, Fall 1985.

Nicholson, S. (ed.), *Shamanism*, Quest Books, Illinois, 1987.

Oesterreich, T., *Possession*, University Books, New York, 1966.

Peters, L. G., 'The Tamang Shamanism of Nepal' in S. Nicholson (ed.), *Shamanism*, Quest Books, Illinois, 1987.

Roth, H. L., *The Natives of Sarawak and British North Borneo* (2 vols.), University of Malaya, Singapore, 1968.

Schultes, R. E. and Hofmann, A., *Plants of the Gods*, Hutchinson, London, 1979.

Sharon, D., 'The San Pedro Cactus in Peruvian Folk Healing', in P.T. Furst, *Flesh of the Gods*, Allen & Unwin, London, 1972.
- (with Eduardo Calderón, Richard Cowan and F. Kaye Sharon) *Eduardo el Curandero*, North Atlantic Books, Richmond, California, 1982.
- *Starhawk, The Spiral Dance*, Harper & Row, San Francisco, 1979.
- *Dreaming the Dark*, Beacon Press, Boston, 1982.

Stone, M., *When God Was A Woman*, Dial Press, New York, 1976.

Sullivan, H.S. *Conceptions of Modern Psychiatry*, Norton, New York, 1953.

Sun Bear and Wabun, *The Medicine Wheel*, Prentice-Hall, Englewood Cliffs, 1980.

Teish, L., *Jambalaya*, Harper & Row, San Francisco, 1985.

Tylor, E., 'Animism', in W. A. Less and E. Z. Vogt (ed.), *Reader in Comparative Religion*, Harper & Row, New York, 1972.

Vasilevich, G. M., 'Early Concepts About the Universe Among the Evenks', in Henry N. Michael (ed.), *Studies in Siberian Shamanism*, University of Toronto Press, Toronto, 1963.

Walker, B. G., *Encyclopedia of Women's Mysteries*, Harper & Row, San Francisco, 1983.

Wasson, R. G., *Soma: Divine Mushroom of Immortality*, Harcourt, Brace Jovanovich, New York, 1968.
- *The Wondrous Mushroom*, McGraw Hill, New York, 1980.

GLOSSARY

AGAPE A love feast usually featuring a common meal with hymns and prayers, from the Greek word for 'love'.

ANIMISM The belief that spirits inhabit everything natural (e.g. animals, rocks, trees), from the Greek word *anima*, meaning 'soul'.

BULL-ROARER An instrument that is swung around the head by a shaman to produce an altered state of consciousness.

CARDINAL POINTS The four main points of the compass: north, south, east and west.

CLAIRAUDIENCE The psychic ability to hear voices and sounds attributed to the deceased.

CLAIRVOYANCE The psychic ability to see discarnate beings and spirits, and to foresee future events.

CLAN MISTRESS The guardian of animal souls, who dwells in the lower world and is consulted about the hunt.

COSMIC RIVER A mighty river joining the three levels of the cosmos and providing the counterpart of the cosmic tree or World Tree.

CURANDERO/CURANDERA In Mexico and Peru, a folk healer or shaman skilled in summoning spirits to heal the sick.

DIVINE DEER Master of the deer species, believed to represent life itself.

DREAMTIME According to Aboriginal tradition, a mythical period during which ancestral beings moved across the Earth, forming its physical features.

FAMILIAR The form (often of an animal) taken on by a spirit to assist a shaman. A familiar is under the shaman's control.

FETISH An object that is believed to have intrinsic magical powers or which is thought to be the embodiment or habitation of a spirit. Fetishes are sometimes considered to have the power to ward off evil.

GHOST DANCE RELIGION A late 19th-century messianic movement among the North American Indians, characterized by a belief in the resurrection of all dead Indians on an Earth free of death and disease.

INITIATION A magical ceremony involving a sense of transition or self-transformation. The subject may be shown new symbolic mysteries, given a secret name or word of power, or granted new ceremonial status.

INTERCARDINAL POINTS The points of the compass in between the cardinal points: north-east, north-west, south-east and south-west.

KACHINA GOD Among the Hopi Indians, ancestral spirits and gods of the clouds, who are impersonated by masked dancers in ritual ceremonies.

KABBALAH The ancient Jewish mystical tradition, based on an esoteric interpretation of the Old Testament. The Kabbalah presents a symbolic explanation of the origin of the universe and has as its central motif the Tree of Life, which links the godhead to the world of creation.

KINGILLI SINGERS Aboriginal singers who believe that the songs they sing are the same as those sung by their ancestors in the dreamtime.

MEDIUMISM A passive action (as opposed to shamanism, which is active) whereby one acts as a receiver of the divine force and is possessed by the spirit of a dead person, becoming their mouthpiece.

MESSIANIC MOVEMENT Any religious movement relating to a Messiah, and a belief in salvation granted through this spiritual leader's teachings or doctrines.

PSYCHOTOMIMETIC A substance that is capable of producing a temporary psychotic state of such intensity that the 'visionary' or 'dream' world seems real. The drug reaction resembles natural forms of psychosis.

SHAKTI In Hindu cosmology, the personification of the creative principle and the consort of Shiva. The term is also used to describe a female partner in Tantric rituals.

SHAMAN'S DRUM An instrument used to create a resonant drumbeat, which 'carries' the shaman to the magical world.

SHAMAN'S RATTLE An instrument used to summon up spirits.

SHAMAN'S SONG The sounds of the gods and spirits, through which the shaman expresses power and intent.

SOUL-BODY The spirit vehicle of the shaman, through which he or she encounters the gods and receives sacred knowledge.

SPIRIT GUIDE An ally of the shaman, who can detect the origins of illness, retrieve lost souls, show a path past obstacles, etc. The spirit guide may appear to the shaman in a dream vision or spontaneously after initiation.

SPIRIT HELPER/GUARDIAN A spirit (often a minor deity or the spirit of a deceased shaman) upon whom the shaman can call for help, but who retains a certain independence and is not directly under the shaman's control.

SPIRIT-JOURNEY The journey undertaken by shamans when they project their consciousness into other realms and return with sacred information for the benefit of a client or the tribe.

TABOO An activity forbidden by the accepted conventions or codes of behaviour in a given society. In shamanic societies broken taboos have to be atoned for by appeasing the ruling deities.

TOTEM ANIMAL An archetypal animal (eg deer, eagle) that is symbolic of the unity of a particular clan and regarded as sacred.

TOTEMIC CLAN UNITY A group of people who are united by their belief in a guardian totem.

TOTEMISM The belief that individual clans are symbolized by a sacred animal or mythic creature.

TRANCE (MEDIUMISTIC) A state of trance in which another entity – a god or spirit – possesses the body of the medium and speaks through it. Mediums have no conscious recollection of what transpires during the state of possession.

TRANCE (SHAMANIC) A state of visionary consciousness characterized by the journey of the soul. The shaman undertakes this journey to obtain information from the gods and spirits and retains full awareness and control of the visionary state.

UNDERWORLD The lower realm of the cosmos, which is regarded as the abode of the dead and is often associated with the spirits of illness and disease.

VISION QUEST A journey of the spirit, undertaken either for personal spiritual renewal, or in order to help heal a 'dis-spirited' person.

VOODOO/VOODOU Haitian magical practices involving witchcraft and trance communication with ancestral spirits. Voodoo is characterized by mediumistic trance possession and to this extent differs from the shamanic journey of the soul.

WORLD TREE The centre of the cosmos (also known as the Tree of Life), the vertical axis between the three worlds (the sky, the Earth where humankind dwells, and the underworld) in which man lives. The shaman can pass up and down this axis, passing effortlessly from one level of existence to another.